THE CASE *AGAINST* PSYCHOANALYSIS

by Andrew Salter

Tнıs brilliant and clearly written book contains some of the most devastating assaults upon the shibboleths of modern psychoanalytic theory and *practice* ever expressed in print.

Andrew Salter's carefully considered opinions on this highly controversial subject are based on the feeling among many psychiatrists and psychoanalysts that psychoanalysis is scientifically discredited, its therapeutic claims highly exaggerated, and, that despite its purported modifications, it still remains an outdated sexual psychology, more riddled with danger than resolution.

The author has this to say of his book:

"Modern psychology has shown Freud's map of the mind to be as inaccurate and

:w World, and practical shown psychoanalytic ısipid and unimpressive

trying to burlesque psy- is unnecessary to do so, done it himself. Are not vulgarization of human lo they not inflate the absurd? . . . There is no to quote out of context. reposterous enough, and reader can fail to note imself provides the evi- utes him.

therapy, of course, can ınd as the theories that ıd since those underlying t only incredible but also herapeutic principles de- m can only be most un- d serve as guideposts on rapeutic futility."

The Case

AGAINST

Psychoanalysis

ANDREW SALTER

The Case

AGAINST

Psycho-analysis

NEW YORK : HENRY HOLT AND COMPANY

ACKNOWLEDGMENTS

I AM glad to express my thanks to the following from whose publications I have quoted:

Boni and Liveright; Cape and Smith, Inc.; Dover Publications, Inc.; Farrar, Straus and Young, Inc.; Grosset and Dunlap; Harcourt, Brace and Company, Inc.; Hellman Williams and Company; Henry Holt and Company, Inc.; Hermitage Press, Inc.; Paul B. Hoeber, Inc.; The Hogarth Press, Ltd., and the Institute of Psycho-Analysis; International Universities Press; Alfred A. Knopf, Inc.; The Macmillan Company; Macmillan and Company, Ltd.; McGraw-Hill Book Company, Inc.; Methuen and Company, Ltd.; W. W. Norton and Company, Inc.; Oxford University Press, Inc.; Perma Giants; Random House, Inc.; Rinehart and Company, Inc.; The Ronald Press Company; Charles C. Thomas, Publisher; University of Chicago Press; William Wood and Company; World Publishing Company.

American Journal of Orthopsychiatry; American Journal of Psychiatry; British Journal of Medical Psychology; Commentary; International Journal of Psycho-Analysis; Journal of Abnormal and Social Psychology; Journal of the American Medical Association; Journal of General Psychology; Look Magazine; The Nation; The New York Times; Psychoanalytic Review; The Saturday Review of Literature; Scientific American; The Sewanee Review; Social Science Research Council.

PREFACE

I HAVE put more work into this little book than I care
to remind myself of. For to undertake to write about
psychoanalysis is to try to relate the history of a kalei-
doscope. I have had to ask myself constantly, "Did
Freud revise this particular statement of his later? And
if he did, did he revise the revision later still? Or,
instead, did Freud follow his propensity to retreat to
a new position, without bothering to give up the old
one?" Since the majority of analysts claim to accept
the basic rules of technique as laid down by Freud,
it is mainly to his writings that I shall refer when pre-
senting the technique of "standard psychoanalysis."[1]

I am fully aware that psychoanalysis is a highly
charged subject, but I certainly have not tried to distort it by an uncharitable selection from the evidence.
Anybody with the time and inclination to gather
together, as I have, and to saturate himself in Freud's
writings, will have to concede that I have been completely fair to the corpus and spirit of Freud's doctrines. Nor would it be any more accurate to hold any
lapses in good taste against me. I have, in fact, passed
over statements of Freud of even greater gaucherie
than those I have found necessary to quote. One may
well doubt this assurance after reading what I have

included. Again I must refer the reader to Freud's collected works. In an effort to facilitate clarity, I have concerned myself in particular with psychoanalytic therapy rather than with Freud's excursions into cultural phenomena.

As I said earlier, this book has been long in the writing. Consequently, though originally prepared for this book, Chapter One in somewhat different form has previously appeared in *Look* Magazine. I want to thank the editors for their permission to reprint it here. And finally, my thanks to my secretary, Elizabeth Lassen, for her help with the innumerable drafts of this little book.

ANDREW SALTER

New York
1952

CONTENTS

The Case

AGAINST

Psychoanalysis

1

THE TWILIGHT OF PSYCHOANALYSIS

By its researches . . . [psychoanalysis] has led to a knowledge of characteristics of the unconscious mental which have hitherto been unsuspected, and it has discovered some of the laws which govern it.[1]

—SIGMUND FREUD

THAT was what Freud said just before he died, after reiterating it all his life. But the truth has turned out to be quite different. Modern psychology has shown Freud's map of the mind to be as inaccurate and wildly fanciful as the pre-Columbus maps of the New World, and practical experience has shown psychoanalytic therapy to be insipid and unimpressive in its results. Consequently, even those who are still practicing its methods have become filled with doubts and are constantly reinterpreting and rewriting the Master's gospel.

There are the Jungians and the Adlerians, the Stekelites and the Reichians, the Horneyites and the

Menningerites, and the so-called Washington and Chicago Schools. Great indeed is the confusion of tongues, for psychoanalysis no longer is the be-all and end-all of therapy, and many psychiatrists and psychologists do not accept its dictates at all.

The free market place of scientific ideas is very cruel. What was yesterday's greatest favorite may be scorned and insulted today. Yet how shall it be otherwise, unless we are to deny ourselves the salutary influence of unfettered thinking in our efforts to attain truth? The first half of this century marked the rise of psychoanalysis—the second half of this century witnesses the twilight of psychoanalysis.

Why has psychoanalysis fallen upon such evil days? Consider the reports of two outstanding psychologists who themselves were psychoanalyzed. Carney Landis is the principal research psychologist of the New York State Psychiatric Institute. Some years ago he underwent a complete psychoanalysis (221 hours' worth) paid for by the Rockefeller Foundation. When it was over, Landis wrote a report.

"What is normality?" Landis asked his analyst one day after the analysis was well under way.

"I don't know," replied the analyst. "I never deal with normal people."

"But suppose a really normal person came to you," Professor Landis asked.

"Even though he were normal at the beginning of the analysis, the analytic procedure would create a neurosis," the analyst admitted.[2]

This is a terrifying admission indeed. Psychoanalysis, apparently, can give you something you didn't have in the first place—a first-class neurosis as a direct result of the treatment.

The experience of Edwin G. Boring, Professor of Psychology at Harvard University, was even more disillusioning. "It is perhaps enough to say," he wrote, explaining why he entered analysis, that ". . . I was depressed, that I seemed to achieve little, that the thought of my professional accomplishment's diminishing rather than increasing in the future seemed utterly intolerable to me. So evident was my emotional disturbance that many of my associates urged analysis upon me, and into psychoanalysis I went, therefore, as a last resource."[3]

But after 168 sessions with his analyst—who incidentally was a friend and pupil of Freud's—Boring reluctantly gave up. "I was sad and distraught, knowing that I had wasted one of the four precious sabbaticals that are due me during my life . . . There is so much about this personality of mine that would be better if different, so much that analysis might have done and did not!"

I must be fair and grant that two failures of psychoanalysis are not at all conclusive. Every form of psychotherapy has its failures—and personally I cannot pretend to cure everyone who comes to me for treatment. Nevertheless, the reactions of two psychologists of the highest professional achievement and reputation cannot be lightly dismissed.

To get any results at all—good, bad, or indifferent—the analyst must dig with the ferocity of a Bantu laborer working deep in a Rand mine. However, the Freudian results are out of all proportion to the herculean effort expended.

To this the psychoanalysts have a ready answer. Therapy is difficult, and results are unimpressive, because human beings are very complicated. Consequently it takes a great deal of effort to achieve a small degree of improvement. This sounds reasonable until we take a good look at the preposterous Freudian theories that underlie psychoanalytic therapy.

Here, briefly, are the fundamental principles that guide the psychoanalyst in the treatment of EVERY man who comes into his office:

1. *Sex underlies everything.* Mr. Jones wrote a story for his high school magazine only because he was sexually frustrated. Now, Mr. Jones collects stamps and is trying to build up his savings account only because he had poor toilet training as a child.

2. *All dreams are fundamentally sexual.* Last night Mr. Jones dreamed that he walked through a gate in the country with his mother. The gate in this dream, to all psychoanalysts, means a woman's sexual organs, probably his mother's.

3. *All psychological difficulties are manifestations of unexpressed sexuality*—"libido" as the Freudians call it. Mr. Jones is afraid of leaning out of tall buildings not because he gets dizzy and is afraid of falling, but because he once surprised his mother in the shower.

4. *ALL boys want to have sexual intercourse with their mothers.* This desire may be conscious, but is usually unconscious.

   ALL boys want to murder their fathers. This also may be conscious, but is usually unconscious. The wish to murder the father and to have sexual intercourse with the mother makes up the so-called Oedipus complex.

5. *The life of the child is fundamentally sexual.* His interest in play and the world is sexual. There is even a "close association between infantile sexuality and excretory functions, and [there is] sexual coloring in the child's relation to its near relatives."[4] So said Ernest Jones, one of Freud's main disciples. And in Freud's own words, "If the child has any sexual life at all, it can only be of a perverse nature."[5]

6. Again in Freud's own words, *"Generally speaking, every human being oscillates all through his life between heterosexual [i.e., normal] and homosexual feelings."*[6] (Italics mine.) This means, then, that all through life, men (and women) fluctuate between desires for normal sex and homosexuality.

These are the Freudian fundamentals. What is more, the psychoanalysts would have us believe that these incredible ideas apply not only to the neurotic individual but also to all normal men and women. At this point I must assure the reader that I am not trying to be flippant or to make a vulgar oversimplification of the Freudian point of view. I have merely stated it accurately—without suppression or misinterpretation.

But disturbing and repulsive as these Freudian fundamentals may sound, we should not draw any hasty conclusions. For do we not know, after all, that the newborn infant is endowed with sexual organs, and surely must have some sexual reactions? And consequently, might it not turn out that some of the Freudian contentions, preposterous as they may appear, are really true? When we have a scientific point of view, we often find ourselves ending up with conclusions that we would never have entertained, if the unflinching pursuit of truth had not forced these ideas upon us. So, for the moment, let us not be too opposed to the extraordinary picture of the masculine mind as painted by the Freudians, and let us pass on to the fundamental principles that guide the psychoanalyst in the treatment of Mrs. Jones.

Sex, of course, underlies everything. Mrs. Jones enjoyed a tap-dancing course at nine years of age, not because she liked to show off, but because she was sexually frustrated. Now Mrs. Jones keeps her old dresses in the back of her closet because of poor toilet training, and she likes to watch television because it reminds her of the time she peeped through a transom.

All dreams are fundamentally sexual. Mrs. Jones dreamed she was wandering through caverns and was impressed with the stalactites hanging from the roof, and the stalagmites reaching up from the floor. These are obviously symbols for the male sexual organ. The fact that she had visited Howe Caverns the week before was merely an excuse for her "unconscious," said the psychoanalyst.

Mrs. Jones didn't realize it, but when she was a little girl she wanted to have sexual intercourse with her father—after murdering her mother to get her out of the way. Now Mrs. Jones is plagued by insomnia, not because she becomes so tense during the day that it takes her most of the night to relax sufficiently to fall asleep, but because she once saw a little boy urinating in the street.

Most important of all, the analyst believes, was the terrible shock Mrs. Jones had when she discovered that she was sexually different from her little brother. She was four at the time. Of this castration fear of Mrs. Jones', the standard *Psychiatric Dictionary* says, "Psychoanalysts are in agreement that the castration complex is universal, appearing in normal and abnormal individuals."[7] Psychoanalysts and their supporters are indeed in agreement—but nobody else agrees with them.

In 1941 the Rockefeller and Carnegie-endowed Social Science Research Council engaged Professor Robert R. Sears of Harvard to make a report for them.[8] Sears studied no less than 166 articles dealing with efforts to *verify scientifically* the Freudian statements about personality.

Sears decided, "The experiments and observations examined in this report stand testimony that few investigators feel free to accept Freud's statements at face value. The reason lies in the . . . [fact that the Freudian method] makes psychoanalysis a bad science."[9] Moreover, said Sears, "perhaps a dozen other theories would provide as good or better explanations" of the facts.[10]

Whenever psychoanalysts are called scientific has-beens, they are quick to say, "Oh, no. You misunderstand us. We have been changing through the years like all the other sciences. Now we don't emphasize sex quite the way we used to. Besides, we use the word 'sex' in a special and broader sense than the coarse usual usage. Also we have added a great deal about 'the death instinct' and 'aggression.' "

It is as easy to nail a custard pie to the wall as to pin

down the Freudian speculations about the "death instinct" and "aggression." As Professor Sears says, ". . . Freud never formalized his theories of aggression or the death instinct in such a way as to make the experimental data particularly relevant."[11] And so it is with most psychoanalytic writing—vague speculations made to appear like facts.

So far we have considered the psychoanalytic theories. What then is done with these incredible speculations?* Are they allowed to gather dust in libraries as a record of one of the many follies that periodically afflict the human race? Not at all. These nightmarish fancies are applied to the treatment of tormented human beings.

In a psychoanalyst's office the patient lies stretched out on a couch, much as in an undertaker's parlor. The patient tells the analyst whatever crosses his mind and tries carefully to remember his dreams. The analyst listens. He tells the patient as little as possible. As the analyst watches the patient digging into his own memories, the analyst looks for one thing alone. *He hunts the incredible nonsense about sexuality and the death instinct called for by psychoanalytic theory.*

As one of my cases put it, "I didn't resent spilling my guts. It was just that it didn't help." He was being unfair. Analysis *has* helped.

"The neuroses are 'cured' by osteopathy, chiropractic, nux vomica and bromides, benzedrine sulfate, change of scene, a blow on the head, and psycho-

---

* Jastrow has said that "the historian of psychology in the future may well regard the great mass of present-day psychoanalytic literature as one of the strangest anomalies and fantastic vagaries of the early twentieth century."[12]

analysis, which probably means that none of these has yet established its real worth in the matter, and surely that psychoanalysis is no specific. Moreover, since many neuroses are self-limited, anyone who spends two years with a patient gets credit for the operation of nature."[13] That was the conclusion of the late distinguished psychiatrist, Dr. Abraham Myerson, after checking the attitudes toward psychoanalysis of 307 neurologists, psychiatrists, and psychologists. More concisely, he said, "I state definitely that as a therapeutic system psychoanalysis has failed to prove its worth."

The followers of psychoanalysis know that their ridiculous fantasies melt into air the moment they are subjected to the harsh light of science. Consequently, Freud introduced his last book by saying, "The teachings of psychoanalysis are based upon an incalculable number of observations and experiences, and no one who has not repeated those observations upon himself or upon others is in a position to arrive at an independent judgment of it."[14] Or, as another analyst said it, "Nobody can really understand what it [psychoanalysis] is all about without having been analyzed."[15]

This "defense is lame and question-begging," said Joseph Jastrow. "It is used by proponents of cults and quackeries . . . Even if I had the proverbial nine lives to live, I should not feel the obligation to devote one apiece to the practice of physiognomy, phrenology, astrology, numerology . . . and Freudian psychoanalysis, in order . . . to indicate the gross and flagrant violations of logic and sanity which they present."[16]

And Professor Richard T. LaPiere of Stanford

University has said that it is preposterous to say that one cannot possibly understand or criticize psychoanalysis because "he has not been inducted into the mysteries of the cult. If one must believe in a system of interpretation before one can test it against reality, that system is necessarily contrascientific."[17]

It is generally believed that a good way to assess a scientific system is to study it by techniques, attitudes, and concepts *external* to it. But the Freudians, as we have seen, insist that this may not be done. Consequently, psychoanalysis, as it talks about its discoveries, is like a dog chasing its tail. It discovers nothing new, only itself, and barks out the great news to the world. This metaphor is frivolous, but it is well sustained.

Why did psychoanalysis catch on so remarkably if it was so utterly unscientific? Well, most important of all was the fact that Freud had a fifty-year head start on Kinsey. The post-Victorian world found Freud's preoccupation with sex most fascinating, and made much of it in writing and conversation—with a few interesting exceptions.

France, for example, with its relatively healthy attitude toward sex, laughed at Freud's bourgeois Viennese daydreams. Thus Freud complained: "Of the European countries, France has so far shown herself the least receptive . . ."[18] and Jankélévitch, translator of the first of Freud's books to appear in French in 1921, prefaces it: "Psychoanalysis, which for over twenty years has produced impassioned discussion and an abundant literature in German-speaking and Anglo-Saxon countries, was until a few months ago known in France only by hearsay, and the majority of those who risked speaking of it at all thought it smart to make fun of it."[19]

And for related reasons, in the sunny climate of Italy analysis also withered. "Italy," said Freud succinctly, "after many promising starts, ceased to take further interest."[20]

But elsewhere, psychoanalysis with its emphasis on sex had a good press. There was a glut of books and articles. Here are some book titles of the first half century:

> *Easy Lessons in Psychoanalysis*
> *Psychoanalysis of the Reformer*
> *Psychoanalysis and Love*
> *Psychoanalysis and Gland Personalities*
> *Psychoanalysis for Normal People*
> *Psychoanalysis in the Classroom*
> *How to Psycho-Analyse Yourself*

This gives the drift. Needless to say, there was also a deluge of more pedantic and pedestrian volumes. But above all, it was the writers who lathered up the public.

Writers as a group are probably among the most neurotic in the population. When word of the new panacea for their troubles with old wives or new books drifted through they went for the treatment in a big way. Many of them were encouraged to write about their analysis as a means of paying for the expensive treatment. A rash of novels, plays, and short stories resulted. Some even wrote lengthy magazine articles embedded with a remarkable variety of rather too-candid clinical detail.

The net result was a public relations campaign that

millions of dollars could not have duplicated. Once analysis became fashionable among the writers, it was a brief step before their more impressionable readers were fretting impatiently in the analysts' busy waiting rooms.

Everybody was being analyzed. "How's your Oedipus complex?" was the password. Even the dead had no peace. Leonardo da Vinci and Napoleon were psychoanalyzed, and Hamlet also got a going over—to say nothing of Moses, about whom Freud wrote a whole book of inaccuracies.

As for religion, to psychoanalysis it also stems from the obscene Oedipus complex. In Freud's words: "God is in every case modeled after the father, and that our personal relation to God is dependent upon our relation to our physical father, fluctuating and changing with him, and that God at bottom is nothing but an exalted father."[21] Further, said Freud, religion is "a parallel to the neurosis which the civilised individual must pass through on his way from childhood to maturity."[22]

Robert Graves puts it well. "The moronic spirit of psycho-analysis has gained control of serious-looking literature, whether the pretended subject is the Elizabethan theater, the exploits of Ghengis Khan, or popular myths. Or even, for instance, the treatment of lumbago."[23]

Actually, Freud made only one contribution. He took the obscenity out of sex, and made sexuality an object of study. He broke down the wall between the bedroom, the living room, and the bathroom. Freud's contribution was the contribution of a great littérateur and propagandist, and his sexually liberating influence on the post-Victorian world merits strong commendation. In the words of Estes, "psycho-analysis in its day made a great contribution, but that contribution has for some time been complete."[24]

Unfortunately, psychiatry and psychology have paid a heavy price for the Freudian sexual revolution, for psychoanalysis has left behind only a dry and sterile wasteland where the hot winds of analytic controversy raise blinding sandstorms. There is no oasis and nothing grows. It is a dead and awesome thing.

Fortunately, modern psychology has much to offer in place of long-drawn-out and anemic psychoanalysis, for a new and healthy psychology has been developing in the laboratories of most of our colleges and uni-versities. Heartened by this thought, let us summon up our strength, and explore the Freudian labyrinths, to see if by chance there is something there—besides dead ends, darkness, and decay.

2

THE DICTATORSHIP
OF THE UNCONSCIOUS

*One might ask me whether and how far I am
convinced of the correctness of the assumptions
here developed. My answer would read that I
am neither myself convinced nor do I ask that
others shall believe them; or, better stated, I
don't know how far I believe them.*[1]

—SIGMUND FREUD

FREUD was putting it mildly. Psychoanalytic theory
violates simple common sense—the kind of sense that
tells morons to come in out of the rain. I know this
is a strong statement, but I ask the reader to bear
with me for a few pages and to decide for himself.
I shall quote Freud directly so that there will be no
doubts in the minds of the credulous and the uninformed. As for those with axes to grind, to them I
can only quote Charcot—at whose feet Freud once
sat. "In the last analysis, we see only what we are ready
to see, what we have been taught to see. We eliminate
and ignore everything that is not a part of our prejudices."

Fundamental to any understanding of women, says Freud, is the fact that "all women feel that they have been injured in their infancy and that through no fault of their own they have been slighted and robbed of a part of their body."[2] "The girl holds her mother responsible for her lack of a penis, and never forgives her for that deficiency."[3] The girl's hatred for her mother, of course, is the start of the Oedipus complex.

"That the girl recognises the fact that she lacks a penis, does not mean that she accepts its absence lightly. On the contrary, she clings for a long time to the desire to get something like it, and believes in that possibility for an extraordinary number of years; and even at a time when her knowledge of reality has long since led her to abandon the fulfilment of this desire as being quite unattainable, analysis proves that it still persists in the unconscious. . . . The desire after all to obtain the penis for which she so much longs may even contribute to the motives that impel a grown-up woman to come to analysis."[4]

But before the girl is old enough to see an analyst, she turns to her father instead. "The wish with which the girl turns to her father is, no doubt, ultimately the wish for the penis, which her mother has refused her and which she now expects from her father."[5] "With the transference of the child-penis wish on to her father, the girl enters into the situation of the Oedipus-complex. The hostility against her mother, which did not require to be newly created, now receives a great reinforcement, for her mother becomes a rival, who gets everything from her father that she herself wants."[6]

This so-called *penis envy* (the term is Freud's) and

the Oedipus complex with which it is linked, were not passing fancies with Freud. He remained unreconstructed to the end. In his last book he wrote, "In females . . . we find that it is the effect of their lack of a penis that drives them into their Oedipus complex."[7]

These speculations become even more preposterous when we realize that it is the analytic belief that EVERY girl suffers from penis envy and from the Oedipus complex (i.e., wanting to murder her mother and have a child by her father). In Freud's words, the female child's "whole development may be said to take place under the influence of her envy for the penis."[8]

The time has come to ask ourselves for what earthly reason Freud uttered these absurdities. Was it all a colossal leg-pull—were these beliefs based on his own daydreams—or were they, after all, founded on solid scientific observation? Freud's answer is not not impressive:

> One has, after all, plenty of opportunity of watching little girls, and one notices nothing of the sort. But the objection cannot be sustained. One can see enough of such things in children, if one understands how to observe them, and, besides this, you must consider how little the child is able to give preconscious expression to its sexual wishes, and how little it can communicate them. We are therefore acting entirely within our rights in studying the subsequent traces and consequences of this emotional field in [adult neurotics].[9]

Consider this passage carefully.

1. Says Freud, there is a special way of observing

little girls—not the usual way, but "if one understands how." To this we can say—well, maybe.

2. Now, even though we observe in this special way, there is *little to see*. For "you must consider how little the child is able to give preconscious expression to its sexual wishes, and how little it can communicate them." Well, where are we now?

3. What we have to do, instead, says Freud, is to study "the subsequent traces and consequences of this emotional field in [adult neurotics]."

In short, it now turns out that there is no point in making observations of children's sexual behavior—for there is little to see, even if you know how to look for it. We "therefore," says Freud, have to study these (unobserved) manifestations of infantile sexuality in adults.

But how trustworthy are adult recollections of almost forgotten childhood memories—*memories of experiences which may never have taken place?* Hardly trustworthy at all, Freud found. "You will remember that interesting episode in the history of analytical research which caused me so many painful hours?"[10] "Under the *pressure of the technical procedure* which I used at that time, *the majority of my patients* reproduced from their childhood scenes in which they were sexually seduced by some grown-up person. With female patients the part of seducer was almost always assigned to their father. I believed these stories, and consequently supposed that I had discovered the roots of the subsequent neurosis in these experiences of sexual seduction in childhood. . . . When, however, I was at last obliged to recognize that *these scenes of seduction had never taken place,* and that they were only phantasies which my patients had made up or *which I myself had perhaps forced upon them,* I was for some time completely at a loss. . . . When I had pulled myself together, I was able to draw the right conclusions from my discovery: namely, that the neurotic symptoms were not related directly to actual events but to phantasies embodying wishes and that as far as the neurosis was concerned psychical reality was of more importance than material reality. *I do not believe even now that I forced the seduction-phantasies upon my patients, that I 'suggested' them.* I had in fact stumbled for the first time upon the *Oedipus complex,* which was later to assume such an overwhelming importance, but which I did not recognize as yet in its disguise of phantasy."[11] (The italics are mine.)

Here indeed is an ever-mounting crescendo of faulty reasoning: Shifting from *special* observation of children to observing "how little" can be observed. Shifting from studying these unobserved manifestations in children, to studying them in adults. Shifting from studying adult memories of childhood seduction, to finding out they had never taken place. And shifting from studying imaginary seductions, to the culminating belief that *every* boy wants to murder his father (and have a child by his mother) and *every* girls wants to murder her mother and have a child by her father—the Oedipus complex. With such an approach to reasoning, and with the Oedipus complex as its point of departure[12] psychoanalysis can only become "curiouser and curiouser." It may have its value for passing an idle hour, but it can hardly be called science.

That Freud was less a scientist than a littérateur can be shown in still another way. We have just noticed how Freud reinterpreted nonexistent seduction fantasies into the equally nonexistent Oedipus complex—and proceeded to build psychoanalysis around it. But what did he say when *others* were forced to reinterpret their findings, as scientists often do? That's quite different, says Freud. Then "one is bound to ask oneself how much of this is due to . . . [a] lack of clearness and how much to lack of sincerity. . . . They are now disputing things which formerly they themselves upheld, and not, moreover, on the ground of fresh observations by which they might have been taught something further, but in consequence of different interpretations of the same observations which make the things they see look different to them now from what they did before."[13]

There may yet remain a reader or two who finds it difficult to believe that the texture of psychoanalytic theory can be as odd as I have made it appear. Let me assure such persons that I have been quite fair. Nevertheless, in an effort to resolve any lingering doubts they may have, let me present to them Freud's ideas on modesty and vanity in women.

Their vanity is partly a further effect of penis envy, for they are driven to rate their physical charms more highly as a belated compensation for their original sexual inferiority. Modesty, which is regarded as a feminine characteristic *par excellence,* but is far more a matter of convention than one would think, was, in our opinion, originally designed to hide the deficiency in her genitals. We do not forget that, later on, it takes over other functions. People say that women contributed but little to the discoveries and inventions of civilisation, but perhaps after all they did discover one technical process, that of plaiting and weaving. If this is so, one is tempted to guess at the unconscious motive at the back of this achievement. Nature herself might be regarded as having provided a model for imitation, by causing pubic hair to grow at the period of sexual maturity so as to veil the genitals. The step that remained to be taken was to attach the hairs permanently together, whereas in the body they are fixed in the skin and only tangled with one another. If you repudiate this idea as being fantastic, and accuse me of having an *idée fixe* on the subject of the influence exercised by the lack of a penis upon the development of femininity, I cannot of course defend myself."[14]

After this, of course, some of Freud's miscellaneous observations on women can only be anticlimactic.

> Her happiness is great indeed when this desire for a child one day finds a real fulfilment; but especially is this so if the child is a little boy, who brings the longed-for penis with him.[15]
>
> The first anxiety experience, of the human being at least, is birth; and this means, objectively, separation from the mother, and could be likened to a castration of the mother (in accordance with the equation: child = penis) .[16]
>
> Even a marriage is not firmly assured until the woman has succeeded in making her husband into her child and in acting the part of a mother towards him.[17]
>
> The only thing that brings a mother undiluted satisfaction is her relation to a son; it is quite the most complete relationship between human beings.[18]

> It must be admitted that women have but little
> sense of justice.[19]

No wonder Freud said, "You are now prepared for
the conclusion that psychology cannot solve the riddle
of femininity."[20] At any rate, not with such preposterous psychoanalytic speculations, which would
be amusing if they were not actually used in psychoanalytic therapy.

As we saw, the trouble with girls, according to
Freud, was that they didn't have a penis. Well, the
trouble with boys, he said, is that they *do*—and they're
afraid that their fathers will castrate them. And he
says this seriously indeed.

Two quotations: "When a boy, from about the age
of two or three . . . feels pleasurable sensations in his
sexual organ and learns to procure these at will by
manual stimulation, he becomes his mother's lover.
He desires to possess her physically in the ways which
he has divined from his observations and intuitive
surmises of sexual life and tries to seduce her by
showing her the male organ of which he is the proud
owner. In a word, his early awakened masculinity
makes him seek to assume, in relation to her, the
place belonging to his father, who has hitherto been
an envied model on account of the physical strength
which he displays and of the authority in which he
is clothed. His father now becomes a rival who stands
in his way and whom he would like to push aside."[21]
It is worth remarking that Freud sometimes called the
Oedipus complex "the family romance," but this has
a distasteful sound, and is usually avoided by analysts.

Said Freud in another place, "In the very earliest

years of childhood (approximately between the ages of two and five) a convergence of the sexual impulses occurs of which, in the case of boys, the object is the mother. This choice of an object, in conjunction with a corresponding attitude of rivalry and hostility towards the father, provides the content of what is known as the *Oedipus complex,* which in every human being is of the greatest importance in determining the final shape of his erotic life."[22]

Please note that the Oedipus complex is alleged to be of *the greatest importance* "in every human being," meaning in both normal and neurotic individuals—*everybody.* And Freud has even said that because of the Oedipus complex there is encountered the so-called womb and rebirth fantasy.[23] There is a wish to be inside the mother's womb in order to replace her during coitus—in order to take her place in regard to the father. . . . There is a wish to be back in a situation in which one was in the mother's genitals; and in this connection the man is identifying himself with his own penis and is using it to represent himself.

At this point I cannot blame the reader if he throws up his hands and says, "Very well. Psychoanalysis is preoccupied with sex. You have established your point. What else?"

To such readers I must say, in extenuation, that I have only been trying to describe some of the fundamentals of psychoanalysis, and also, that difficult as it may be to believe, there are some analysts who have denied that sex is fundamental to their theories. I must say that these analysts, whatever their status, may well be accused of being somewhat ignorant, or perhaps even hypocritical. Menninger, however, is a refreshing exception. He at least has met the objections to analytic sexuality frankly and head on. He writes, "It happens that Freud used the word sex as being inclusive of much more than genital activity. This, and the fact that American usage of the word is much more restricted explains some of the resistance to psychoanalysis. Moreover, the American cultural taboo is a significant factor contributing to a high incidence of neuroses."[24]

I am somewhat perplexed at this point of view. Surely penis envy is rather genital, the castration complex is rather genital, and the Oedipus complex, which lies at the heart of psychoanalysis, is genital indeed.

As for saying that Freud's use of the word *sex* has been misunderstood because of certain of its more common connotations, Jung's comment will suffice: "Of course any Freudian will assure you that he does not mean coarse sexuality, but 'psycho-sexuality'—an unscientific and logically unjustifiable extension."[25] In fact, Jung once wrote to Freud from America, telling him "of winning friends by soft-pedaling the sexual factor in psychoanalysis. This piece of intelligence . . . infuriated Freud."*

But to get back to Menninger. He is quite correct when he says that national attitudes toward sex have something to do with the occurrence of neurosis. But for that matter so do attitudes toward self, toward people, and toward success—to name just a few. Freud is quite clear. "Among the causes of and occasions for neurotic complaints sexual factors play an im-

* H. W. Puner, *Freud, His Life and Mind* (New York, Grosset and Dunlap, 1947), p. 126. This is a thorough and fearless biography.

portant, an overweening—even perhaps a specific—
rôle."[26] Or much earlier, "What we call the *character*
of the person is built up to a large extent from the
material of sexual excitations."[27]

Once, when Freud felt particularly maltreated at
being constantly reminded of his preoccupation with
sex, he lashed back at his critics by accusing them of
being abnormal. "I know, of course, that the recognition we afford to sexuality is—whether they confess
it or not—the strongest motive for our opponents'
hostility to psychoanalysis. But are we to let ourselves
be shaken on that account? It only shows us how
neurotic our whole cultural life is, when people apparently normal behave no differently from neurotics."[28] This is a strange form of scientific argument,
but it has been supplemented by some of his more
ardent advocates. At one time or another they have
accused their "opponents" of pornography, scientific
pretensions, and dangerous half truths. Actually, of
course, these criticisms apply best of all to themselves.

I have not been trying to burlesque psychoanalysis.
It is unnecessary to do so, for Freud has done it himself. Are not his theories a vulgarization of human
nature, and do they not inflate the banal into the
absurd? Freud was painstakingly thorough, and it is
all on the record. There is no need to lie or to quote
out of context. The truth is preposterous enough, and
no observant reader can fail to note that Freud himself
provides the evidence that refutes him.

But how, you might ask, could anyone have taken
these speculations seriously? Freud accomplished this
by locating his grotesqueries in a vague place called

the "unconscious." After all, since no one can possibly know (without an analyst's help) what goes on in the unconscious, who can deny the possible existence there of the most incredible witches' sabbaths? As Kanner[29] says, "You ignorant mother think that, when the baby sucks at the breast or drinks from the bottle, he does it merely to get some milk. The interpreters of the G. G. U. [Great God Unconscious] know better. The baby indulges in 'sexual activity not yet separated from the taking of nourishment.' His 'sexual aim consists in the incorporation of the object into his body.'[30] The baby is passing through the oral or—you guessed it—cannibalistic phase of pregenital organization." The word "cannibalistic" is Freud's.

Cannibalism had a fascination for Freud. He says, for example, "The idea of being eaten by the father belongs to the typical primal stock of childhood ideas."[31] And on another occasion, "The dread of being *eaten* I have so far found only in men; it is referred to the father, but is probably the result of the transformation of oral aggressive tendencies directed upon the mother. The person the child wants to devour is the mother who nourished him."[32]

But the child, to be sure, is not conscious of these impulses. They exist only in his "unconscious." And what is this "unconscious" anyway? Let Freud give his answer: ". . . we call 'unconscious' any mental process the existence of which we are obliged to assume."[33] (Notice the word "assume.") "There is no need to characterize what we call *conscious:* it is the same as the consciousness of philosophers and of everyday opinion. Everything else that is mental is in our view *unconscious*."[34]

Now, just as the Freudians have tried to rewrite history when it comes to the sexual basis of analysis, so have they tried to reinterpret Freud's contentions about the "unconscious." In the last paragraph Freud ever wrote, he said, "The concept of the unconscious has long been knocking at the gates of psychology and asking to be let in. Philosophy and literature have often toyed with it, but science could find no use for it. Psycho-analysis has seized upon the concept, has taken it seriously and has given it a fresh content."[35] The fresh content, of course, is the content of penis envy, castration complex, cannibalism, and the Oedipus complex.

This position, of course, is difficult to defend, so the analysts, fighting as they retreat, have declared, "Say what you will, Freud brought to the foreground the fact that our behavior is determined by the unconscious." To put it charitably, this is simply not so. James, Prince, Janet, Carpenter, Delboeuf, and Holmes, to name just a few, all wrote in great detail about unconscious activity. The contribution of psychoanalysis was the *sexualization of the unconscious*. To speak loosely of the unconscious as being made up of such instincts as the individual possesses, and such habits as he has acquired from his environment, is the solution of common sense, and is, in fact, the solution of modern psychology. Our hearts beat, our lungs breathe, our stomachs digest, all quite unconsciously. Life would be quite impossible without this "unconscious." But Freud did not say that behavior was determined by the unconscious. What he said was that behavior is determined by the unconscious and *the unconscious is the untrustworthy home of mysterious Oedipus complexes, cannibalistic urges, death instincts, and homosexual desires in everybody*.

As one psychoanalytic reviewer put it, Freud "brought to light the dark underworld of the unconscious, proving that every symbol and syllable is significant, and revealed how shallow the structure of Victorian common sense had been." Let me assure the gentleman that there is nothing wrong with common sense. It only looks peculiar when you stand on your head.

Maier,[36] on the strength of considerable research, concludes that his findings force him "to question the free use of the concept of the subconscious. . . . In psychoanalytic theory the subconscious is used as a mechanism in behavior and it finds its greatest use in explaining abnormal behavior. . . . If the concept of the subconscious is to be used as an explanatory mechanism, it would seem that it should be more than a reservoir of directions and unrecalled memories . . ." And that, we must remember, happens to be what the Freudians think it is.

Unconscious, preconscious, and conscious—that was how Freud had once classified mental life. We can visualize this in the form of a three-man totem pole, with the low man called *Unconscious*, the one squatting on his shoulders called *Preconscious*, and the high man *Conscious*. That had been the Freudian picture of the mind. But this totem pole soon became badly weatherbeaten, so right next to it Freud set up another three-man totem pole. This added to the confusion. As Freud's disciple Ernest Jones said, "It will not be quite easy to combine the two pictures thus obtained, for the classification is in some respects a crossed one."[37]

On the new totem pole the low man was called the *id*. He is a horrible-looking creature, for he represents the *primitive animal basis* of the human being. Nevertheless, it is "The power of the id [that] expresses the true purpose of the individual organism's life."[38] "The core of our being . . . is formed by the obscure id."[39]

Middle man on the totem pole is the *ego*. He sits on the shoulders of the id. "The severest demand upon the ego," says Freud, "is probably the keeping down of the instinctual claims of the id."[40] This is a difficult task indeed, for "The impulse desires which are born anew with *everybody* are those of incest—cannibalism —and lust of murder."[41] The ego is just the "organized part of the id,"[42] and "On the whole the ego has to carry out the intentions of the id."[43] And considering the fact that the id, the low man on the totem pole, is a "cauldron of seething excitement,"[44] the ego needs help in keeping him repressed.

Freud provides this help by weighing down the ego with a high man on the totem pole—the *super-ego*. If all this seems too ridiculous, I can only tell the reader what Freud said about the ego: "The ego can take itself as object, it can treat itself like any other object, observe itself, criticize itself, and do Heaven knows what besides with itself."[45]

At any rate, balanced precariously on top of the ego sits the super-ego. He has a blue nose and a righteous air. He is the voice of convention, prohibition, and thou-shalt-not. In the case of the neurotic

individual, the "Super-Ego deals with his ego like a
strict father with a child, and his idea of morality
displays itself in primitive ways by making the Ego
submit to punishment by the Super-Ego. Illness is
employed as a means for this 'self-punishment.' The
neurotic has to behave as though he were mastered
by guilt, which the illness serves to punish, and so to
relieve him."[46] All in all, the super-ego's "chief function remains the *limitation* of satisfactions."[47]

Let us walk with a flashlight into the dark Freudian
graveyard and take an inventory. In the darkness
loom the two totem poles—the totem of consciousness,
and the totem of id levels. Deeper in the graveyard
are Freud's five mortuary statues—pairs of wrestlers
grappling with each other, the so-called *polarities:*

1. *Eros* vs. *Thanatos: life* wrestling with *death*. There
   is an inscription saying that this is also called
   Love vs. *Hate.*
2. *Activity* vs. *Passivity.* This statue is battered and
   broken, and remains only out of courtesy to the
   past.
3. *Self* vs. the *Outer World.* These wrestlers are sub-
   titled *Subject* vs. *Object.*
4. *Pleasure* vs. *Pain.* Pleasure looks ecstatic, and has
   pinned down Pain, who is grimacing horribly.
5. The last polarity has Adam wrestling with Eve—
   and is otherwise called *Masculinity* vs. *Femininity.*

Freud said nonchalantly of these "systems": "Such
ideas are part of a speculative superstructure of psycho-analysis, any portion of which can be abandoned
or changed without loss or regret the moment its
inadequacy has been proved."[48] Depending upon the
reality to be analyzed, or the dream to be interpreted,

or the motive to be ascribed, the analyst has but to look through the graveyard and take his choice. One can call the totem poles and statuary many different names, but surely not "science."

". . . if one proceeds to a sufficiently abstract level . . . ," says Schafer,[49] "one reaches a point where all things are true of all people; that is to say, we all have impulses or aspects of impulses which may be characterized as oral or clinging, anal or possessive, homoerotic, narcissistic, exhibitionistic, repressive, projective, hostile, and the like. The life of a human being is so complex that by the proper selection or interpretation one can set out, if he wishes, and find behavior items to confirm almost any interpretation."

All this makes highly suspect any of the reports alleging laboratory proof of Freudian hypotheses. As Sears concluded, after making his classical *Survey of Objective Studies of Psychoanalytic Concepts,*[50] "the further analysis of psychoanalytic concepts may be relatively fruitless so long as those concepts rest in the theoretical framework of psychoanalysis."

Freud's conception of evidence will surprise the reader who is accustomed to thinking that evidence means proof. "Castration," he says, "has a place, too, in the Oedipus legend, for the blinding with which Oedipus punished himself after the discovery of his crime is, *by the evidence of dreams,* a symbolic substitute for castration."[51] (Italics mine.) The evidence for the Oedipus complex is less than nil, yet Freud drags in "the evidence of dreams" in its support.

Freud, in fact, was even wrong about the Oedipus myth in the first place. Mullahy, in his thoroughgoing book on the subject, says,

1. "In all except one of the older versions of the myth [Oedipus] does not marry his mother at all.[52]

2. "Another question: since Oedipus is the courageous and wise hero who defeats the Sphinx and is therefore the benefactor of Thebes, why is he the man who commits the crime which is considered to be the most horrible by his contemporaries?[53]

3. "Westermarck[54] [an anthropologist of the highest repute], after submitting Freud's notions about the Oedipus complex to a long searching examination, concludes that the 'facts which have been adduced in support of the supposed prehistoric events to which Freud has attributed the inhibition of incest have thus in each case been found to be worthless as evidence.'[55]

4. "Fromm claims [and this interpretation, at least, makes some sense] 'that the [Oedipus] myth has to be understood not as a symbol of the incestuous tie between mother and son, but as the rebellion of the son against the authority of the father in the patriarchal family. . . .' "[56]

I shall not present any of the evidence showing how completely wrong Freud was in declaring that the Oedipus complex was true of *all people, in all places, at all times*. No one seriously contends this any more. Instead, various well-meaning souls have tried to transform the incestuous, murderous, and symbolically castrated Oedipus into a good citizen. This they have tried to do by spraying him with a bland anthropological mist. Like this, for example: "This means," says Bateson,[57] "that the constellation into which the child is born, the Oedipus situation which he encounters, varies profoundly from culture to culture."

Now, in these "enlightened" days, we all know that family life reflects aspects of the environment in which it finds itself. This is a well-established fact, and I grant that it is worthy of intensive study. But subtly to extend the Oedipus complex into a synonym for the study of child development and family life is, as Jung said of Freudian psychosexuality, "an unscientific and logically unjustifiable extension."

Freud made himself quite clear as to what he meant by the Oedipus complex, and he was completely wrong. We have nothing to gain by using his concepts. More generally, it is confusing, and I think it is poor method, for persons to interpret their findings in *old Freudian terms into which they have injected new and variable meanings*. This policy results only in the confusion and degradation of psychology.

Despite these comments on psychoanalytic terminology, I nevertheless think it is unfair to accuse the analysts of writing in a private gobbledygook. Though their language often brings to mind a cryptographic code, their specialized vocabulary is actually saying something. That something may be dubious, but nonetheless it is a specific set of ideas and amenable to discussion.

There is even meaning in the following passage, taken from Freud's *Outline of Psychoanalysis*. The jacket of this book hails it as "A masterpiece of clarity and conciseness." I think the reader will find the passage heavy going:

> This factor exercises a decisive influence upon the outcome of the conflict when a boy finds himself in the situation of the Œdipus complex and the

threat aimed against his narcissism by castration, reinforced from primeval sources, takes possession of him. Driven by the combined power of these two influences, of the immediate real danger and of the remembered phylogenetic one, the child embarks upon his attempts at defense (repressions), which are effective for the moment but nevertheless turn out to be inadequate when the later reanimation of sexual life brings a reinforcement to the repudiated instinctual demands.[58]

Put more clearly, what Freud was really saying was that: "This factor is decisive when a boy is in the Oedipus situation. In the first place there is an apparently real danger of castration at the hands of his father. And in the second place, the boy's inherited knowledge also warns him of this threat. Driven by these two forces, the boy tries to thrust his dangerous sexual desire for his mother into his unconscious. He succeeds for the moment, but later, when his sexual life reawakens, his repudiated sexual demands come to the fore again." With this passage I have not tried to show that I am a better translator (or paraphraser) of Freud than is James Strachey. Rather, I have tried to show that when we rob analytic writing of its intimidating vocabulary, we are usually left with shabby and defenseless speculations.

I must grant, however, that one of Freud's most preposterous theories had a real basis in truth. But I must add that, despite this, he succeeded in distorting it so thoroughly that it has become one of his most pernicious doctrines. I am referring to his theory of the death instinct.* Put simply, "The goal of all

* Opposed to the "death instinct," Freud put a life instinct. His calling it "Eros" serves to remind us that it is sexuality renamed.

life is death."[59] Human beings—all living matter, in fact—have an *inborn tendency* to die, and in one way or another are *trying* to die.

Of course, it is one thing to say that all living things must die. It was said adequately over two thousand years ago. "Man that is born of woman is of few days, and full of trouble. He cometh forth like a flower, and is cut down; he fleeth also as a shadow, and continueth not."

But when Freud says that living matter *instinctively aims for death* he enters the realm of pseudo-biology, where there is no evidence at all—only rhetoric. The consequence is that his elaboration of his death instinct theory is so laborious that even his sympathetic disciple, Ernest Jones,[60] was constrained to remark that it "calls for special indulgence on the part of the reader. On account, doubtless, of the extreme complexity and remarkable novelty of the ideas . . . the style is one of exceptional difficulty."

Freud's "thoughts on the ultimate problems of life" are tragicomic. He talks of "sexual instincts active in every cell that take the other cells for their 'object' [and], partially neutralise their death-instincts . . . while other cells do the same for them, and still others sacrifice themselves in the exercise of this libidinous function. The germ cells themselves would behave in a completely 'narcissistic' fashion, as we are accustomed to describe it in the theory of the neuroses when an individual concentrates his libido on the ego . . . Perhaps the cells of the malignant growths that destroy the organism can also be considered to be narcissistic in the same sense."[61] I think even the most rabid psychoanalyst will be hard put to restrain a grin at this.

But it becomes a horrible mockery of life and of logic when Freud says, "These circuitous ways to death . . . would be neither more nor less than the phenomena of life as we now know it . . . the whole life of instinct serves the one end of bringing about death."[62] One might well think that, to Freud, day was a circuitous way of attaining night. And as for the belief that there are instincts of self-preservation, why, says Freud, "they are part-instincts designed to secure the path to death peculiar to the organism . . . the organism is resolved to die only in its own way."[63]

Much nonsense has been written about instinct, and I must say, not just by Freud alone. Morgan underlines this in his standard text on physiological psychology. "The principle most often followed . . ." Morgan[64] says, "is that of calling any behavior instinctive which is somewhat complicated and *whose mechanisms are not understood by the observer*. Instinctive behavior, therefore, gets defined in terms of the ignorance of the observer." And Bernard[65] could well have been thinking of the contemporary Freudians when he said, "More popular uses of the term instinct . . . still freely persist among littérateurs and publicists, who usually come in contact with scientific criticism only indirectly and frequently a generation or more after it has been made."

A good illustration of how our knowledge of instinct has been transformed is provided by the salmon. The point is important and not uninteresting. In Freud's day some biologists believed that "When certain fish undertake arduous journeys at spawning-time [they do so] in order to deposit the spawn in certain definite waters far removed from their usual habitats."[66]

We know now* that "The young salmon, in the waters where it has been born, gradually loses the pigmentation in its skin which serves to protect photosensitive receptors below this pigmentation . . . With loss of this pigment, the fish is stimulated by light and reacts negatively, that is, avoids light. Since the upper streams are shallow, this light-avoidance reaction takes him gradually down stream to the deep ocean where he is free from photic stimulation. Because the waters of the river emptying into the ocean are somewhat colder, contain somewhat more oxygen, and are less salty, the salmon tends to stay in the general region of the ocean into which the river runs."

I shall skip a few details and simply say that as the salmon matures it undergoes changes in hormone activity. This leads the salmon "to the choosing of colder waters, much as the sexually mature bird chooses colder climates, and also raises the requirements for oxygen . . . The fish then heads upstream, and as it comes to each branching of the river, it chooses the one which is of the colder temperature. This has been established by measurements of the temperature chosen by salmon in their upstream migration. . . ." All this is rather disillusioning about the salmon, and about instinct, but it makes instinct a part of science, rather than of folklore and pseudo-science.

Instinct, then, is not a nebulous force of some mysterious kind. Rather, instinct involves a *specific*

* I have taken this explanation from Morgan.[67] His entire chapter "Instinct" is most enlightening.

response by an organism. And this *specific* response is brought out by *specific* factors from the environment or from the organism itself.

More technically, an instinct, we know now, is

1. A specific inherited response,
2. Which follows or accompanies an
3. Inner or outer stimulus
4. That serves to release this response.[68]

In the light of contemporary knowledge, therefore, we can say, without the slightest possibility of contradiction, that Freud's theory of the death instinct is without the remotest basis in fact whatever.

What calls for further comment, though, is that Freud's theory of the death instinct was not based on fact even in the days when he hypothesized it. At that time there was some scientific belief that an instinct was something inherited from primitive ancestors, and that it helped organisms to get along with their environment. What Freud did was to drop the part about *adapting to the environment,* and say solely that instinctive behavior was *primitive* behavior. In his own words, "an instinct would be a tendency innate in living organic matter compelling it towards the reinstatement of an earlier condition."[69] (Not an earlier condition of *adaptation*—just an *earlier* condition.) Death, of course, and "inertia in organic life" are earlier conditions of existence.

So it was with good reason indeed that Freud said: "This conception of instinct strikes us as strange." It was strange science when he said it, and it is even stranger science now. All that remains true is that man is born to die—which was true even before Freud put his hand to the problem. In the words of J. L. Grey,[70]

". . . the fact that we all die is no proof that we purpose to die, any more than that we are all conceived
is proof of a purpose in nonexistence to become life."

Freud[71] said specifically that the concept of the
death instinct did not "entail a modification of the
psycho-analytical theory of instincts." Freud made no
fundamental change in his recipe. The psychoanalytic
cake remains completely sexual. Only a few scattered
raisins of death instinct and aggression have been
added.

The implications of Freud's thinking, of course,
are quite pessimistic. We all unknowingly search for
death, and are spasmodically held back by the efforts
of Eros. And all the while, deep within us, seethes
an inferno, for ". . . we have to destroy other things
and other people, in order not to destroy ourselves,
in order to protect ourselves from the tendency to
self-destruction."[72] It is not a very pretty picture, for
psychoanalysis is not a very pretty theory. It is in fact
a very unsound theory, and its implications are as
unsound—and as unhealthy—as its original premises.

By now we can understand the famous remark of
Karl Kraus, whom Freud[73] once liked and called "a
witty writer." But that was before Kraus[74] said, "Psychoanalysis is the disease it purports to cure."

3

THE BITTER FRUIT

. . . the testimony of our experience *. . . is that we must not be surprised if the difference between a person who has not and a person who has been analysed is, after all, not so radical as we endeavour to make it and expect and assert that it will be.*[1]

—SIGMUND FREUD

THIS extraordinary admission, made by Freud in the last years of his life, is an incredible verification of the bitter fruit that analytic theory has borne. And if Freud himself had such a low opinion of analytic treatment, we must ask ourselves how seriously we may take the loud claims of his followers. Not very seriously, indeed.

Psychoanalytic therapy, of course, can only be as sound as the theories that underlie it. And since those underlying theories are not only incredible but also unsound, the therapeutic principles derived from them can only be most unsatisfactory, and serve as guideposts on the road to therapeutic futility.

The Freudians have a great deal to say about Genesis, but they are very weak on Exodus. For when it comes to therapy, as opposed to theory, they have to stand up and deliver. And here, no amount of propaganda, apology, explanation, or excuse can turn black into white and convince the uninitiated plebeians that the operation was successful, but the patient died. In psychotherapy people either get better, or they do not, and it happens quickly, slowly, or not at all. Everything else is detail, and is of no interest to the patient, however significant it may be to the therapist.

Analysis, such as it is, takes time. "To speak more plainly," said Freud,[2] "psycho-analysis is always a matter of long periods of time, of six months or a year, —or more—a longer time than the patient expects. . . . I hold it to be altogether more honourable, and also more expedient, to draw his attention, without alarming him unduly but from the very beginning, to the difficulties and sacrifices involved by analytic treatment; thereby depriving him of the right to assert later on that he had been inveigled into a treatment the implications and extent of which he did not realize."

And more recently, one of the leaders of the Freudians, L. S. Kubie, made an even more discouraging statement. Kubie said (and I have italicized some of his words) that analysis "usually requires *at least five sessions each week,*" and "one measures the duration of adequate treatment *in terms of years.*"[3] Of course, it is easy enough to say that human behavior is quite complicated, and that this explains the necessity for the long duration, the anguish, and

the uncertainty of analytic therapy. But I think that
such an explanation overlooks, among other things,
the unquestionable derivation of psychoanalytic practice from psychoanalytic theory. I believe that the
complete inadequacy of psychoanalytic theory is of
itself quite sufficient to account for all the distressing
characteristics of psychoanalytic therapy. But we must
give the analysts their due. They do not misrepresent.
All that they will promise the patient is that the treatment will be long and expensive, and the results will
be uncertain.

The couch is the psychoanalyst's operating table,
for it is there that the patient lies while his heart
undergoes surgery. I suppose that I have put it too
picturesquely, but the fact is that the analysts do insist that their treatment is the most fundamental form
of psychotherapy that is humanly possible.

The couch, like the therapy that goes with it, is a
relic of the past. As Freud[4] said, "it is the last vestige
of the hypnotic method out of which psycho-analysis
was evolved; but for many reasons it deserves to be
retained. The first is a personal motive, one that
others may share with me, however. I cannot bear to
be gazed at for eight hours a day (or more)."

What Freud was referring to was not any possible
defect in his own personality, but to the fact that he
did not wish his "expression to give the patient indi-
cations which he may interpret or which may influence him in his communications." Though some
analysts may use a couch to dramatize their therapy,
I think it is nevertheless true that the couch is a valid
and logical part of analytic treatment. Once we assume that guidance to the patient is to be kept at a

minimum, and that the production of information by the patient is to be assisted by relaxation and un-impeded by the analyst's reactions, it becomes possible to consider the couch as a pertinent psychoanalytic fixture.

But as Fromm-Reichmann[5] has said, "I am giving away no secret when stating that there are therapists who fall asleep while they are supposed to listen, especially if they sit behind their patients and they do not see each other. There are even rationalizations on the part of psychiatrists for such unforgivable errors in procedure—such as 'I only fall asleep if the patient produces irrelevant material and wake up as soon as the patient's productions become relevant.' "

Personally, I have encountered a case where the patient stopped talking when he realized that the analyst had fallen asleep. The silence caused the analyst to awaken, and the analyst said "Yes?" The patient replied, "You were just sleeping." The analyst answered, "Our relationship has just entered a critical phase." This remark was actually one of the longer conversations between analyst and patient in the six months that the patient had been under treatment. The analyst was unable to redeem himself, for the patient stopped seeing him.

But by and large, the analyst listens as intently as he can, and with all the antiseptic objectivity he can muster. "The physician," said Freud, "should be impenetrable to the patient, and, like a mirror, reflect nothing but what is shown to him. . . ."[6] "I cannot rec-ommend my colleagues emphatically enough to take as a model in psychoanalytic treatment the surgeon who puts aside all his own feelings, including that of human sympathy."[7] I suppose that what Gumpert has called a "deeply humane and imaginative relationship to the patient" never hurt anybody, but that is out of bounds for the psychoanalyst. It is forbidden, for it is contended that it more often than not interferes with the treatment. I think this position is indefensible for many reasons. I shall only mention that there is an increasing belief that an inability to *get involved* with people is the fundamental problem of the emotionally distressed. And certainly, any experiences of warmth, human kindness, and "contact" in the therapeutic situation could therefore only conduce to effective treatment. But the analysts say, "No. An attitude of detached awareness on the part of the analyst is best for the patient in the long run." This puts one to mind of "What man is there of you, whom if his son ask bread, will he give him a stone?"

What manner of man, for that matter, is the psychoanalyst anyway? Landis[8] has given us a good description. "Usually the analyst is a physician who has been attracted into psychiatry with little or no knowledge of formal or academic psychology or of philosophy. He knows little and cares less about studies of learning, maturation, and emotional expression. Education and educational methods are to him a closed book. Unless he is a most unusual man, he has had but little time for literature and the arts. His training in science and the scientific method is that of the skilled technician, most of whose training has been of the follow-directions variety. He has been told over and again that psychology and philosophy are the bunk, and that all there is to education and educational method a high school girl of slightly less than average intelligence can grasp in two years.

"Feeling the need of some positive therapeutic procedure with which to approach the pressing problems of the mental patients, or hearing that analysis is a wide-open field offering rich financial returns, he enlists for an analysis and such training courses as may be required to qualify him for analytic society membership. In these training courses he finds he must believe or else . . ."

I shall not talk any more of the analyst's training, but I want to mention that we cannot ascribe much significance to the fact that the analyst has himself been previously psychoanalyzed. Even Kubie,[9] who is not given to underestimating the value of psychoanalysis, has admitted, "The fact must be faced, . . . that in spite of the therapeutic purpose of the training analysis its therapeutic leverage is not as great as that of the analytic process when it deals with patients. Perhaps it is fair to say that in training we often start with an individual *who is more than usually vulnerable to emotional stress,* and try to make him less vulnerable than the average. . . . It is not surprising that the training process does not always attain this goal . . ." (Italics mine.) Nevertheless, Kubie concludes, "From the point of view of the patient, however, it is essential only that these residues of earlier neurotic difficulties shall not under any circumstances interfere with the analyst's objective attitude towards his patient's problems or with his therapeutic relationship to the patient himself."

In my opinion, I think that it is impossible for an analyst to keep his own inadequacies from harming the patient. I have spoken of this elsewhere, and I cannot do better than to repeat myself.[10] "There is no greater obscenity than an inhibitory psychiatrist, for he cannot help rationalizing his patients in terms of his own emotions. Nobody is exempt from the laws of the human nervous system. It may be objected that in order to examine a broken rib under the fluoroscope, it is immaterial whether the physician has ever personally sustained such an injury. This analogy is not well taken. In psychotherapy, the fluoroscopic screen is the therapist. That is his instrument for studying the patient." Old Mother Hubbard found the cupboard was bare—so the poor dog went hungry. The analyst cannot give the patient what he himself does not possess. *Nemo dat quem non habet.* No one can give what he hasn't got.

The analysts answer this with Freud's words: "So far as possible we refrain from playing the part of mentor; we want nothing better than that the patient should find his own solutions for himself."[11] In Glover's words, "The essential remodelling must be done by the patient."[12] The psychoanalysts have apparently overlooked the implications of their position, for what they have said is that they have put the therapy in the hands of the sickest man in the office—the patient. It is my conviction that the therapist should be extremely active at all stages of treatment, but I shall touch on this somewhat later in the book, at a point where it is more relevant.

For the moment, then, I shall just quote Myerson. "I know most of the distinguished psychiatrists of America," he said, "and the distribution of wisdom and wise living among them is about equal to that in the general population."[13] Surely, we cannot expect the sincere, psychoanalytically trained technician to be any better. The psychoanalyst is a man, like other men. He has gone to school and has learned what he has been told. He is only as strong as the ideas he advocates, and his ideas, as he sits quietly out of sight of his unhappy patient, are only the ideas of psychoanalysis.

The psychoanalysts compare their procedures with those of the archaeologists, and talk of excavating the unconscious, and discovering and freeing its repressed material. I would like to suggest another and more appropriate metaphor that also deals with digging. Analytic therapy, I think, is actually more like "salting" a mine. The analyst sprinkles and buries false nuggets of Oedipus, castration (or penis envy), and bisexuality. Then, as the patient digs (where he is directed to dig) and discovers the planted material, the analyst is convinced that he has struck pay dirt. I think that any archaeologist who, under cover of darkness, buried spurious relics in order to unearth them the next day, would hardly be considered honorable. Yet the analysts do precisely this, quite sincerely and in open daylight. For it is by *suggestion* that the analysts implant their preposterous "discoveries" in the minds of their patients, and it is by *suggestion* that the patient is taught to find what he never possessed in the first place.

"The mechanism of our curative method," says Freud, "is indeed quite easy to understand. We give the patient the conscious idea of what he may expect to find . . . and the similarity of this with the repressed unconscious one leads him to come upon the latter himself."[14] Let us go over this with some care, for Freud says that it is nothing less than "the mechanism of [his] curative method."

The analyst, says Freud, has to "give the patient the conscious idea of what he may expect to find." It seems to me that if the analyst tells the patient what he may expect to find, it is splitting hairs to conclude that the patient finds it "himself." And how could a patient, by *himself*, possibly find what he was told to find if the idea he was looking for is a "repressed unconscious one"? When an idea is "repressed" and "unconscious," then by definition it cannot possibly be recognized by the patient as an idea the analyst is seeking. Only the analyst would be able to recognize an idea as akin to one he had suggested to the patient.

Now, if a patient can appraise neither his own "unconscious" material nor the analyst's contentions about it, it certainly appears as if the patient lies completely anesthetized on the analyst's couch and is completely at his mercy. I think there is nothing wrong in a patient being at a surgeon's mercy. But the patient has a right to expect, among other things, that the surgeon is going to operate on him with modern and sterilized instruments, and not with some rusty Victorian museum pieces.

When a patient is frightened and vulnerable (which is why he goes to a psychoanalyst) and when a patient is subjected to two hundred or more hours of psychoanalytic processing (as he usually is), his desperate desire to try anything in order to get better can easily result in his believing that not only does he have an incestuous desire for his mother but also for his grandmother. Does the reader doubt that a boy can have an incestuous desire for his grandmother? Freud's English ambassador, Ernest Jones, has no doubts.

"With *very many* children there is a lively desire to become the parents of their own parents. . . . This curious construction of the imagination . . . is evidently closely connected with incestuous wishes, since it is an exaggerated form of the *commoner desire* to be one's own father."[15] (Italics mine.) Comment on this passage would only be superfluous.

The patient has come to analysis because he does not understand himself. Consequently, what is more natural than that he defer to the "superior" knowledge of the analyst and accept the Freudian interpretations that are so persistently and mechanically advanced? Wortis has described Freud's annoyance at being told that one of his interpretations seemed farfetched, and how Freud "would wait until he found an association which would fit into his scheme of interpretation and pick it up like a detective at a line-up who waits until he sees his man."[16] Patients are not morons, but in psychoanalysis they are out of their depth, and they soon discover, however obliquely, that the analyst prefers that they talk about some things and not about others.

And what happens when a patient is recalcitrant and asks difficult questions? "When we are further along, you'll understand," the analyst would tell Carney Landis,[17] whose futile experience with analysis we saw in Chapter One. Since 99 per cent of patients are less informed psychologically than Professor Landis, we may conclude that it is easy enough for an analyst to keep a patient at arm's length.

Since the analysts believe that *every* person suffers from an Oedipus complex and castration fear (or penis envy), why, we might ask, do they not communicate this intelligence to every patient at his first session, and save him a good deal of time and money? "You do not understand," the analysts would answer. "It is not enough simply to tell these things to a patient. The important thing is for the patient to *work through* his repressed material." This has a plausible sound, until we ask, "Work through *what* repressed material?" And then it becomes clear: The repressed material is the Oedipus complex, the castration complex, and the other fictions that the analysts have manufactured in the first place. For in psychoanalysis, *all roads lead to Oedipus and the castration complex,* no matter where the patient may start.

The analysts go to such great pains to compare their efforts to archaeological excavation that their pretensions necessitate further comment. "In a psychoanalysis," says Freud, "the physician always gives his patient the conscious expectation-ideas by the help of which the patient is put in a position to recognize that which is unconscious and to grasp it." We recall this formulation a bit earlier. But this time Freud continued, "On one occasion the physician gives this help more plentifully and on another less.* There are some cases that require more assistance and others that require less. But without such help nobody comes out [of psychoanalysis]."[18]

Notice this last sentence. "But without such help

* This sentence, emphasizing the analyst's role, is omitted from the official English translation.

nobody comes out [of psychoanalysis]." The "personal influence of the analyst . . . ," said Freud, "does exist, and plays a big part in the analysis."[19] "This personal influence is our strongest dynamic weapon . . ."[20] Freud is specific enough. "We serve the patient in various functions as an authority and a substitute for his parents, as a teacher and educator . . ."[21]

Here, then, is a definite contradiction in Freudian theory. We saw earlier that the analyst is supposed to be silent and objective—and here is the analyst using pressure and influence. How can the analysts reconcile these opposing viewpoints? There is no contradiction at all, they answer. Psychoanalysts *always* try to be objective—an effort which I think is worthy but impossible. As for being silent, versus directly influencing the patient, well, the patient will have to trust the analyst's judgment.

The psychoanalyst is in a difficult position. He runs the risk of being either a silent fumbler or a wordy dispenser of Freudian platitudes applied by rote. But whatever policy he follows, it will not matter very much to the patient. The facts he reveals to the analyst will be constantly reworked and reshaped and processed and cut and molded to fit the preposterous psychoanalytic principles that dominate the therapy.

For we know that a man is not a psychoanalyst just because he gives an ear to people's soliloquies, any more than a man is a historian because he scribbles down facts about a nation. The facts about a nation, or an individual, have significance only when they are carefully selected, and have been interpreted by means of certain theories and hypotheses. There is no such thing as pure history existing in a vacuum. The analyst, then, both deliberately and without meaning to do so, is selecting facts and interpreting facts (already distorted by the patient's memory) to fit the psychoanalytic hypotheses. And what is more, to quote Cohen and Nagel, "The function of hypotheses is . . . not less important because they are implicit or employed tacitly."[22] Each man knows a thing only in his own manner of knowing it.

When the Freudians say that they are studying the history of an individual, they are doing no such thing. What they are doing is giving a psychoanalytic interpretation to the history of an individual. Psychoanalysis can make no discoveries in the individual. It can only discover itself. In the words of Landis, psychoanalytic "phenomena are as much a result of method and procedure as of any basic personality structure revealed by the method."[23]

For some time I have been pressing the point that the psychoanalytic method is closely related to suggestion. This relationship, I think, is a logical outgrowth of the fact that Freud worked with hypnosis for years, and studied with Charcot and Bernheim. "The importance of hypnotism for the history of the development of psychoanalysis," said Freud, "must not be too lightly estimated. Both in *theoretic as well as in therapeutic aspects* psychoanalysis is the administrator of the estate left by hypnotism."[24] (Italics mine.)

I think that Freud, as "the administrator of the estate left by hypnotism," should be brought before some celestial Surrogate for an accounting, for he did the same thing to hypnotism that he did with everything else—he made it sexual. Hypnotism, he said, was based on "sexuality, on the functioning of the libido."[25] And what is more, the *only way* to cure patients was to influence them by this *sexualized suggestion.*

Let me repeat this, because I want to emphasize it: the psychoanalysts are of the opinion that the *only way* to cure patients is to influence them by sexualized suggestion—*transference,* as they call it. "The attitude [of transference]," said Freud, "is, in fact—to put it bluntly—a kind of falling in love."[26] "Psychoanalysts," says the authoritative *Psychiatric Dictionary,* "consider that transference is basically concerned with the displacement of matters of infantile sexuality upon the physician."[27]

Before going into some of the ramifications of transference, I want to remark that the popular belief that one has to fall in love with one's psychoanalyst in order to get better is apparently not the product of patients' hysterical imaginations. Rather, this belief is a product of analytic theory and procedure and reflects the psychoanalytic preoccupation with sex. I must emphasize that I am not contending that psychoanalysts are interested in exploiting their patients sexually. I am saying, however, that the idea of *transference* is highly dangerous nonsense.

For without the transference, a patient, however ill, would hardly believe the incredible interpretations the analyst advanced to him. ". . . In so far as his transference bears the positive sign, it clothes the physician with authority," said Freud, and "transforms itself into faith in his findings and in his views. Without this kind of transference or with a negative one, the physician and his arguments would never even be listened to . . . Without this support arguments have no weight with the patient."[28] "The neurotic sets himself to the work because he believes in the analyst, and he believes in him because he begins to entertain certain feelings toward him."[29] Transference has an "all-important, absolutely central significance.[30] An analysis without transference is an impossibility."[31]

Now we can see more clearly why the patient, lying on the couch, gives serious attention to the analyst's incredible ideas. The patient, to put it bluntly, has been hooked by the transference. Now he will believe anything. He will even believe the psychoanalytic interpretation of dreams, which is truly "sound and fury, signifying nothing." But analytic dream interpretation is something else again, and I shall devote the entire next chapter to it.

4

PSYCHOANALYTIC DREAM INTERPRETATION

The more one is occupied with the solution of dreams, the readier one becomes to acknowledge that the majority of the dreams of adults deal with sexual material and give expression to erotic wishes.[1]

—SIGMUND FREUD

DREAM interpretation is absolutely fundamental in psychoanalytic theory and practice. Freud said that "the interpretation of dreams is the royal road to a knowledge of the unconscious,"[2] to the unconscious of the psychoanalysts, at any rate.[3] And Landis[4] reported that his analyst spent 30 per cent of the time on his dreams and his associations with them. He was lucky. Most analysts consume even more time on dreams. Freud summarized it to a patient one day. "I have been waiting up to now to see if you would tell me of your dreams, because from now on the real analysis begins."[5]

I think it best, for the sake of orderly development,

to start with a straightforward explanation of Freudian dream theory. Then, after I have fully described it, I will proceed to my own comments on what I consider the inadequacy of the analytic position. What follows, therefore, for some paragraphs, is an accurate and completely impartial explanation of the psychoanalytic theory of dreams.

To the psychoanalyst, dreams have both a *manifest* and a *latent* content. The manifest content is what the dream is obviously about. The latent content is what the dream is secretly about. In order to determine the real meaning of the dream, it is necessary to remove the mask worn by the latent content. This the analyst does by asking the individual to say everything that comes to his mind about the dream. These personal associations of the dreamer are carefully untangled, and the analyst gradually discovers the underlying wishes of the individual.

The analysts say further that the latent content of a dream may disguise itself in many ways. Thoughts from the unconscious may become transformed and enter dreams as their opposites: in a dream a mother may stand for a father and a house may stand for an office. Unconscious wishes and impulses may also follow this law of contraries and appear in dreams as the reverse of themselves. Love, for example, may appear as hate, and hate, in a dream, may be love in disguise. Frequently the unconscious takes the associations of words and plays with them and changes them before letting them appear in a dream.

In general, the content of dreams is distorted by what Freud called the unconscious *censor*. Unpleasant ideas are banished from consciousness and are kept repressed deep in the unconscious. In dreams these repressed ideas surge up and enter the consciousness of the dreamer. Dreams are the expression of unfulfilled wishes that the dreamer wants to satisfy. Even sensory stimuli from the outside world get distorted according to the inner wishes of the individual. An unmarried young woman dreams of the ringing of wedding bells as her alarm clock rings; this is a clear form of wish fulfillment. Dreams protect sleep, says Freud, for they permit repressed impulses in the unconscious to attain satisfaction.

Freud further says that dreams are basically neurotic, and their absurdities and delusions parallel those of the insane. Dreams are also regressive, that is, dreams relate back to the earlier life of the individual. The unconscious wishes expressed in dreams usually stem from childhood, and so do most of the personal associations that an individual has to his dreams. This personal symbolic language is usually sexual, but not always, and often much of the symbolism found in dreams has nothing to do with the individual's personal experiences. Rather, the symbolism was his at birth and was inherited from his prehistoric ancestors.

There. That is the Freudian interpretation of dreams, and as you can see, I have kept my promise not to interrupt it with comments and criticisms. But now I am no longer bound by my promise, and I shall proceed to a discussion of the fallacies and misapprehensions that underlie analytic dream theory.

First, the Freudian myths are no truer at midnight than they are at noon. The same Oedipus complex castration complex, and related fictions are used in interpreting sleeping behavior as are used in interpreting waking behavior. These fictions remain without any foundation whatever.

As for the additional hypotheses with which Freud saddled dream interpretation, they too are also quite unsound. For example, he postulated a "censor" working in the brain, permitting some ideas to enter the consciousness of the dreamer without interference, permitting other ideas to get through only after they were disguised, and repressing still others into complete oblivion. Said Freud, "I regard the attribution of dream-distortion to the censorship as the central point of my conception of the dream."[6] Analogy is not proof, and though the feats of the Freudian censor make interesting reading, they are only analogies, doubly compounded.

The transmutation of manifest content into latent content is another speculative hypothesis. As we shall see, the so-called manifest content of a dream, with a little imagination, can be converted into hosts of meanings, every meaning different, and most of them inconsistent with each other.

Secondly, psychoanalytic dream theory is riddled with faulty logic and repeated inconsistency. I shall give just a few illustrations.

At one point Freud says, "This *regression* [i.e., this going back to earlier recollections] is therefore assuredly one of the most important psychological peculiarities of the dream-process; but we must not forget that it is not characteristic of the dream alone."[7] Now how can *"peculiarities"* of the dream process also be *"characteristic"* of something else? The answer, of course, is that Freud's important peculiarity is neither important nor peculiar. It is just a statement, meaningless, inconsistent, and obscure.

Sometimes, however, Freud just utters a complete falsehood and proceeds to build on it. "Every dream," he said, "is an attempt to put aside a disturbance of sleep by means of a wish-fulfillment."[8] "The dream is the guardian of sleep, not its disturber."[9] The fact is that every single iota of experimental psychological evidence completely negates these statements. Dreams hinder sleep. Dreams, whether pleasant or unpleasant, always have a negative effect upon the restorative value of the dreamer's slumber. There is hardly anyone who has not tossed through a night disturbed by dreams and awakened in the morning weary and unrested. Dreams are *not* the guardian of sleep. Dreams are the enemy of sleep.

Or again, Freud agrees that outside stimuli (noises, for example) can cause a sleeper to dream. But, he says, though the noises start the dream, they "cannot be held responsible for the content" of the dream.[10] That is true enough. But it is just a flat statement to say that the dream "still remains a wish-fulfilment, no matter how its expression is determined by the actual material available."[11] What happens outside the dreamer is undebatable, but what happens within the dreamer is Freudian conjecture. Whenever a psychoanalyst has a fact he can't explain, he modifies it with a hypothesis he can't prove.

Thirdly, it is not at all true that "In every dream an instinctual wish is displayed as fulfilled."[12] Freud's

circular logic is particularly flagrant here. He re-
peatedly assumes as proven the very point he has
neglected to prove, and uses these groundless statements as a means of "explaining" dream phenomena.

We have all had dreams that were distinctly disturbing and unpleasant. How can such dreams possibly be called wish fulfillments? Well, says Freud,
some "persons may have counter-wish-dreams and disagreeable dreams, yet these are for them nothing more
than wish-fulfilments, which satisfy their masochistic
inclinations."[13] Masochistic inclinations are present in
some people, but surely not in everybody. How can
a painful dream in which the dreamer is punished be
a wish fulfillment? Easily enough, says Freud. "It is
just as if one said: 'If I take the punishment on myself, then I can do the forbidden thing.' "[14] Take your
choice. You punish yourself in order to punish yourself, because you're a masochist; or you punish yourself in order to reward yourself, because you are
pleasure-seeking. This is vicious reasoning.

And if the individual punishes himself in his dream
and never does the forbidden thing, what then? "The
dream is an *attempted* wish-fulfilment."[15]

Freud has further circular logic to "prove" his
contention that even punishment dreams and anxiety
dreams are wish fulfillments. The reader will recall
the *super-ego* as one of the many Freudian formulations. Well, says Freud, sometimes the critical super-
ego expresses its stern wishes in a dream, and this
makes the individual unhappy. That's all there is to it:
a painful dream can be a super-ego dream. Freud
could possibly be right—that is, if there *were* a super-
ego, and dreams *were* wish fulfillments, and wish ful-

fillments *were* both masochistic and nonmasochistic, and substituting one unknown for another could masquerade as explanation.

The student who dreams of failing before the final examination, the girl who dreams of losing her panties at the graduation dance, or the criminal who dreams he has been arrested—they are all dreaming dreams that have meaning, but to take positive or negative wish fulfillment ideas as methods of interpreting them is complete idiocy.

What happens when one dreams of the death of a loved one, and no amount of perverted logic or imagination can twist it into a wish fulfillment? How does Freud explain such a dream? It is still a wish fulfillment! "Wherever a wish-fulfilment is unrecognizable and disguised [Freud ignores the possibility that there may be no wish fulfillment present] there must be present a tendency to defend oneself against this wish, and in consequence of this defence the wish is unable to express itself save in a distorted form."[16] Freud is saying, in essence, "When an analyst can't find a wish-fulfilment in a dream, the analyst *knows* it's there, 'in a distorted form.' " If one drilled for oil according to Freudian principles, the drier the hole the surer one would be that oil was present "in a distorted form." Those who would say that there was no oil would be accused of being scientifically uninformed.

Sometimes, said Freud, what looks like oil may really be water, and what you think is water may really be oil. "One meaning or one wish-fulfilment may conceal another."[17] This makes the anarchy of wish fulfillment complete. Anything can stand for anything else . . .

Freud once realized that he was cornered by some contradictions in wish fulfillment theory. He made no effort to escape. He just shrugged his shoulders and said, "How is it possible for me then to contradict myself [in the face of certain objections] and assert [nevertheless] that dreams are always and only wish-fulfilments? I do it rather than permit a stupid misunderstanding which might cost us the fruit of all our labours on the subject of dreams."[18] What fruit? What labors? The fruit is spoiled and the labors are wasted. Rather than give up his theory—as a scientist would—Freud preferred to hang on to his contradictions.

But by now I think the reader has wearied of the bombast of psychoanalytic wish fulfillment. At any rate I have, and I shall proceed, without further ado, to my next objection.

My fourth point is that it simply is not true, as Freud said, that "A dream is itself a neurotic symptom,"[19] nor is it any truer to say that ". . . the dream is a pathological product. The state of sleep represents a turning away from the real external world, and thus provides a necessary condition for the development of a psychosis."[20] "A dream, then, is a psychosis, with all the absurdities, delusions and illusions of a psychosis. No doubt it is . . . harmless and even performs a useful function. . . . Nevertheless it *is* [Freud's italics] a psychosis."[21]

Professor Calvin S. Hall "has collected more than 10,000 dreams thus far, not from mental patients but from essentially normal people,"[22] which verify everybody's common-sense knowledge that perfectly happy, normal people dream. Their dreams may differ from those of neurotics, but normal people do dream, and often too.

Freud makes normal dreaming abnormal in another way. ". . . in their essentials [the processes of dream formation] reveal the closest analogy with the processes observed in the formation of hysterical symptoms."[23] * And he implies something quite similar when he says that not only do dreams stem from suppressed wishes, but so do neurotic symptoms. ". . . it can only be sexual wish-impulses from the infantile life, which have undergone repression . . . which . . . supply the motive-power for all psychoneurotic symptom-formation."[24]

I have devoted space to the somewhat obvious point that dreams are not neurotic, and I have done so for what I consider good and sufficient reasons. The analysts would have us believe that their profane fictions are the psychology of normal everyday life. If the Oedipus and the castration complex are normal, abnormality is probably a state to be preferred.

My fifth objection to the psychoanalytic interpretation of dreams is that *it is inaccurately and preposterously sexual.* Jones has registered distress at the people who say this. "In point of fact, however, in his [Freud's] theory there is no necessary connection at all between dreams and sexuality . . . the wish-fulfilment by means of which the dream is constructed

---

* Yet he illogically continues this passage by saying, "Now the dream is not a pathological phenomenon."

need not be sexual, though, it is true, *it most often is.*'[25] (Italics mine.) Personally, I would say that Freud's emphasis on the sexual basis of dreams may be valid for some people, at some time, in certain circumstances—but that is not what the Freudians are saying at all.

Freudians know no innocent dreams. "Dreams which are apparently guileless turn out to be the reverse of innocent if one takes the trouble to interpret them; if I may be permitted the expression, they all show 'the mark of the beast.'[26] . . . dreams which are conspicuously *innocent* commonly embody crude erotic wishes . . ."[27] Says Freud further, ". . . we find from analysis that the majority of dreams—innocent dreams, dreams without affect [that is, without feeling] and anxiety dreams—are revealed, when the distortions of the censorship have been undone, as the fulfilments of immoral—egoistic, sadistic, perverse or incestuous—wishful impulses. . . . The straightforward dream of sexual relations with one's mother . . . is a rarity in comparison with all the multiplicity of dreams which psycho-analysis must interpret in the same sense."[28] "I can assure the reader that disguised dreams of sexual intercourse with the dreamer's mother are far more frequent than undisguised dreams to the same effect. There are dreams of landscapes and localities [Freud continues] in which emphasis is always laid upon the assurance: 'I have been here before.' But this '*Deja vu*' has a special significance in dreams. In this case the locality is always the genitals of the mother; of no other place can it be asserted with such certainty that one 'has been here before.' "[29]

To me this is nauseating, and I think that my previous writings protect me from the accusation of being "old-fashioned."

Freudian dream interpretation is based upon an incredible code book of symbols. This code book, by means of which the analysts endeavor to interpret their patients' dreams, has so often been denied that I shall quote enough detail to make its essence absolutely incontrovertible. Here is what Freud says about dream symbols. [The brackets and paragraphing are mine.]

"The number of things which are represented symbolically in dreams is not great. The human body as a whole, parents, children, brothers and sisters, birth, death, nakedness—and one thing more. The only typical, that is to say, regularly recurring representation of the human form as a whole is that of a *house*. . . . When the walls are quite smooth, the house means a man; when there are ledges and balconies which can be caught hold of, a woman.

"Parents appear in dreams as *emperor* and *empress*, *king* and *queen* or other exalted personage; in this respect the dream attitude is highly dutiful. Children and brothers and sisters are less tenderly treated, being symbolized by *little animals* or *vermin*.

"Birth is almost invariably represented by some reference to *water:* either we are falling into water or clambering out of it, saving someone from it or being saved by them, i.e., the relation between mother and child is symbolized."[30] "When in a dream a man rescues a woman from the water, it means that he makes her a mother, which in view of the considerations discussed above means that he makes her his own mother. When a woman rescues someone else (a child) out of the water, she represents herself as the mother who bore him, like Pharaoh's daughter in the Moses legend.

"The phantasy of rescuing the father will also occasionally have a tender meaning. It then expresses the wish to have the father for a son, that is, to have a son like the father. . . . I do not consider it necessary to advance any justification for my method of working out my observations . . ."[31] [Indeed!]

"People who dream often, and with great enjoyment, of *swimming,* cleaving the waves, etc., have usually been bed-wetters, and they now repeat in the dream a pleasure which they have long since learned to forgo."[32] [Is the reverse true? Do people who enjoy swimming have an unconscious desire to wet their beds?]

"The male genital organ is symbolically represented in dreams in many different ways. . . . In the first place, the sacred number three is symbolic of the whole male genitalia. [Let me assure the reader that Freud is quite serious.] Its more conspicuous and, to both sexes, more interesting part, the penis, is symbolized primarily by objects which resemble it in form, being long and upstanding, such as *sticks, umbrellas, poles, trees* and the like; also by objects which, like the thing symbolized, have the property of penetrating, and consequently of injuring, the body,—that is to say, pointed weapons of all sorts: *knives, daggers, lances, sabres;* fire-arms are similarly used: *guns, pistols and revolvers,* these last being a very appropriate symbol on account of their shape.

In the anxiety-dreams of young girls, pursuit by a man armed with a knife or rifle plays a great part. This is perhaps the most frequently occurring dream-symbol: you can now easily translate it for yourselves. The substitution of the male organ by objects from which water flows is again easily comprehensible: *taps, watering-cans, or springs;* and by other objects which are capable of elongation, such as *pulley lamps, pencils which slide in and out of a sheath,* and so on. *Pencils, penholders, nail-files, hammers* and other *implements* are undoubtedly male sexual symbols, based on an idea of the male organ which is equally easily perceived.

"The peculiar property of this member of being able to raise itself upright in defiance of the law of gravity, part of the phenomenon of erection, leads to symbolic representation by means of *balloons, aeroplanes,* and, just recently, *Zeppelins.* [Freud's illustration is dated, and so is his theory.] But dreams have another, much more impressive, way of symbolizing erection; they make the organ of sex into the essential part of the whole person, so that the *dreamer himself flies.* Do not be upset by hearing that dreams of flying, which we all know and which are often so beautiful, must be interpreted as dreams of general sexual excitement, dreams of erection."[33]

"Nor must you think to object to this on the ground that women can also have dreams of flying; you should rather remind yourselves that the purpose of dreams is wish-fulfilment, and that the wish to be a man is frequently met with in women, whether they are conscious of it or not. . . ."[34] [This is a neat piece of sophistry.]

"But why do so many people dream of flying? Psychoanalysis answers this question by stating that . . . the wish to be able to fly signifies in the dream nothing but the longing for the ability of sexual accomplishment. This is an early infantile wish . . . Thus aviation, which has attained its aim in our times, has also its infantile erotic roots."[35] [Let me remind the reader once more that Freud is serious.]

"Male sexual symbols less easy to understand are certain *reptiles and fishes:* above all, the famous symbol of the *serpent.* Why *hats and cloaks* are used in the same way is certainly difficult to divine, but their symbolic meaning is quite unquestionable. . . ."[36]

"The female genitalia are symbolically represented by all such objects as share with them the property of enclosing a space or are capable of acting as receptacles: such as *pits, hollows and caves,* and also *jars and bottles,* and *boxes* of all sizes, *chests, coffers, pockets,* and so forth. *Ships* too come into this category. Many symbols refer rather to the uterus than to the other genital organs: thus *cupboards, stoves* and, above all, *rooms.* Room symbolism here links up with that of houses, whilst *doors and gates* represent the genital opening. Moreover, material of different kinds is a symbol of woman,—*wood, paper,* and objects made of these, such as *tables* and *books.* From the animal world, *snails and mussels* at any rate must be cited as unmistakable female symbols; of the parts of the body, the *mouth* as a representation of the genital opening, and, amongst buildings, *churches and chapels* are symbols of a woman. You see that all these symbols are not equally easy to understand.

"The breasts must be included amongst the organs

of sex; these, as well as the larger hemispheres of the female body, are represented by *apples, peaches and fruit* in general. The pubic hair in both sexes is indicated in dreams by *woods and thickets*. The complicated topography of the female sexual organs accounts for their often being represented by a *landscape* with rocks, woods and water, whilst the imposing mechanism of the male sexual apparatus lends it to symbolization by all kinds of complicated and indescribable *machinery*. . . .

"Gratification derived from a person's own genitals is indicated by any kind of *play*, including playing the piano. The symbolic representation of onanism by *sliding or gliding* and also by *pulling off a branch* is very typical. A particularly remarkable dream-symbol is the *falling out* or *extraction of teeth*; the primary significance of this is certainly castration as a punishment for onanism.[37] [Let dentists and patients beware.] I will not assert that the interpretation of dreams due to dental stimulus as dreams of masturbation (the correctness of which I cannot doubt) has been freed of all obscurity. I carry the explanation as far as I am able, and must leave the rest unsolved."[38] [Freud adds a footnote:] "According to C. G. Jung, dreams due to dental stimulus in the case of women have the significance of parturition dreams. E. Jones has given valuable confirmation of this. The common element of this interpretation with that represented above may be found in the fact that in both cases (castration-birth) there is a question of removing a part from the whole body."[39]

"Special representations of sexual intercourse are less frequent in dreams than we should expect after all this, but we may mention in this connection rhythmical activities such as *dancing, riding* and *climbing,* and also *experiencing some violence, e.g.,* being run over."[40] ". . . stairs, steps and ladders in dreams, . . . are certainly a symbol of coitus. The underlying element which the two things have in common is not difficult to discover; one climbs an acclivity in rhythmic movements, accompanied by increasing breathlessness, and in a few rapid leaps can be down below again. Thus the rhythm of coitus reappears in climbing steps."[41]

"A *tie,* being an object which hangs down and is not worn by women is clearly a male symbol, whilst *underlinen* and *linen* in general stands for the female,"[42] etc., etc.

Freud's sexual preoccupation, so apparent in the passages I have just quoted, has been denied by him. Why, he said, "I have never maintained the assertion which has so often been ascribed to me that dream-interpretation shows that all dreams have a sexual content or are derived from sexual motive forces."[43] "The assertion that *all dreams call for a sexual interpretation* is quite foreign to my *Interpretation of Dreams.*"[44] And curiously, despite my wealth of evidence, Freud is correct in his denial—*literally* correct, but no more. For Freud did not ascribe a sexual interpretation to "all dreams"—he only gave a sexual interpretation to *almost* "all dreams." This is a fine distinction, but it is a valid one. Nevertheless, it is quite deceptive.

When Freud said that "hunger, thirst, or the need to excrete, can produce dreams of satisfaction just as well as any repressed sexual or egoistic* impulse,"[45] he seemed to have forgotten that he once wrote: "The nature of the dream is not altered when somatic [i.e., bodily] material is added to the psychic dream-sources; it still remains a wish-fulfilment, no matter how its expression is determined by the actual material available."[46] Bodily sensations in sleep, to the psychoanalysts, act as triggers which liberate repressed unconscious wishes. There is that psychoanalytic dodge again. Undebatable bodily facts get converted into unprovable psychoanalytic fictions.

It has been said by some of his critics that Freud's sexual symbols reveal more about Freud than they do about his patients. Much as Freud's thinking is distasteful to me, I think that this is an unfair criticism, for scientifically speaking the only point that matters is whether Freud's sexual symbolism is true or not. Jones, whom we will recall as one of Freud's key disciples, "states that dream symbolism . . . [is] exclusively sexual. The reason for this, he says, is still unknown."[47] I think we can suggest the reason. Freudian dream symbolism is "exclusively sexual" because Freud's invasion of the night is based on the same fictions as his invasion of the day. It is all preposterous, and it is all of a piece.

My next objection to psychoanalytic dream interpretation is that it makes for *many and completely divergent interpretations of the same dream*. As Schafer said, "There is as a rule quite a bit of variation of emphasis if not outright disagreement in the field, even when those concerned are numbered

---

* I shall discuss Freud's sexualization of egoistic impulses in my next chapter.

among the more orthodox Freudians."[48] Now this is a serious objection indeed. Freud was once asked, "How does one ever know if a dream is correctly interpreted?" His answer was, "All interpretations are tentative."[49] I would say that all interpretations are highly dubious.

At this point I could tell how obviously Freud interpreted the dream of:

- —a girl who dreamed that "She puts a candle into a candlestick; but the candle is broken, so that it does not stand up,"[50]
- —a young woman who dreamed that she wore "a straw hat of peculiar shape, the middle piece of which is bent upwards, while the side pieces hang downwards,"[51] or
- —a woman who dreamed that "She is climbing down from a height over a curiously shaped trellis, and she is glad that her dress doesn't get caught anywhere,"[52] etc.

As I said, I could tell how Freud interpreted these dreams, but it should be quite obvious by now. Or then again, by going into laborious detail, I could show how fallacious were Freud's pat explanations of those same dreams. But working this way could result in my being accused of having insufficient evidence, of selecting from previously selected data, and of just plain reading between the lines. And considering Freud's technique of dream interpretation, these criticisms might well be true.

I think, however, that I have overcome these objections. For I have found a dream which one psychoanalyst presented for interpretation to two other psychoanalysts, and I shall present their two divergent interpretations. I am quoting Lorand,[53] an analyst who teaches psychoanalysis to other analysts.

"One of the physicians being supervised by me, presented the following dream brought in by one of his patients:

> My friend M. (a sickly young man) is crossing the street. He has on a hat and he is smiling.

"His patient's associations brought out the following main ideas: M. (the friend) is constantly cared for by his mother, even to the extent that she knows of the prostitutes who visit him and encourages him to receive them. Everyone in M.'s home is subservient to him because of his illness. In contrast, the patient is always made to feel at fault by the constant criticism of all the members of his family, especially his mother. His main symptoms are exhibitionism, voyeurism, and impotence. Other associations of the patient concern arguments in his home a few days earlier which led him to compare himself with M., noting how much better off his friend was.

"On the basis of the associations, the dream seemed to me to indicate the following: M. is carelessly crossing the street, happy, unconcerned about the onrushing traffic. He is behaving like a carefree child, whom everyone has to help and give attention. He can do no wrong. The traffic on the streets must stop when he crosses. He can expose himself (exhibit his sexuality) without shame or fear, like a happy child. Having his hat on and smiling referred to the patient's wish to exhibit his penis, and his enjoyment of the activity. Throughout this dream the patient identifies himself with his friend, M. who is so happy and carefree, whose mother gives him every attention, and who can exhibit his sexuality without fear.

"After the dream had been interpreted for the analyst in the control hour, he later presented it at a seminar on dreams led by another training analyst, who explained it differently. This colleague emphasized the homosexual component. According to his interpretation the dream expressed the patient's homosexuality: M. is a woman with a penis, and crossing the street smilingly means he is a prostitute. The student claimed that the seminar leader rejected all other approaches or explanations."

One interpretation makes the young man's hat a sign of masculinity, and the other interpretation calls the young man nothing less than "a woman with a penis." Analysts, apparently, take Freud seriously when he said, "Of many dreams it may be ascertained, by careful interpretation, that they may even be understood bisexually, inasmuch as they yield an indisputable over-interpretation, in which they realize homosexual impulses—that is, impulses which are contrary to the normal sexual activity of the dreamer."[54] Lorand does not tell us if either or both of these interpretations was relayed to the unhappy patient. Nor does he seem to be convinced of his own opinion either, for he says, "Although these two interpretations differ widely, both have validity and may describe the content of the patient's unconscious."[55] I think, though, that we can say for Lorand's interpretation that it is less ridiculous and more in touch with reality than is that of his colleague, but it is still tarred by the same Freudian brush. It is also worth asking what happens to the patient when one analyst teaches his training analysts one point of view, and another analyst teaches them an opposing point of view. The answer is that the patient gets lost in the shuffle of opposing fictions.

The dream we have just been considering, with its two conflicting interpretations, also illustrates something else. Please note that before the dream was interpreted, the teacher wanted to know the patient's *personal* associations—which sounds like an intelligent idea. Nevertheless, after getting those same *personal* associations, both analysts made certain *selections* from them, and then proceeded to transmute those selected associations into the Freudian fool's gold. Personal associations have meaning, but the Freudian viewpoint corrupts them all. Freud says it quite specifically. "Although in dream-interpretation we are in general and predominantly dependent on the associations of the dreamer, nevertheless we treat certain elements of the content quite independently . . . and long experience has taught us that they are to be taken as *symbols* for something else."[56] Here, just when it would seem that Freud (in Dryden's words) "deviates into sense," Freud reverts to his standard sexual symbols, and we are right back where we started. In general, the attention given by analysts to their patients' dream associations is particularly dangerous, for it deludes the patient into thinking that the interpretations advanced have been based on a study of his own personality. Actually, the patient's personal associations have had their individuality bleached out in the Freudian lye vat.

In point of fact, any two ideas, at first thought completely unrelated, can be brought together by only two, or at most three, associations. Freud has said that, "We are right in supposing that the longer and the more circuitous the chain of associations, the stronger is the resistance."[57] I would say it is an absence of ingenuity and imagination on the part of the analyst that makes the associations long and circuitous, sometimes going into a half-dozen steps. If a man is not a dullard, he can get from A to Z in two or three jumps.

In an effort to give a demonstration of this, I opened a dictionary at random, and my finger fell upon the word *fungi.* I decided to take the singular, *fungus,* and wrote it down on a piece of paper. A few moments later, a man I was treating entered my office and sat down. I said to him, without any preparation whatever, "Please tell me a word—any word."

Said he, "Any word?"

"Yes, any word."

He thought for a while and then said, "Pronoun."

I wrote *pronoun* down, and explained that I was trying to see if it were possible to go from any word to any other word in no more than two intermediate steps.

I looked at *fungus,* and I looked at *pronoun,* and then I had it.

> Fungus obviously Latin
> Latin—high-school courses and Roman history and Proconsul—and then why not
> Pronoun.

An hour later I did it just as logically,

> Fungus—obviously Latin
> Latin—a high school course, as opposed to English

English—grammar and such
Pronoun.*

Oh no, the analysts object. These ingenious link-
ages may be possible, but it is the associations brought
forth by the patient's unconscious that really matter.
We want the patient's unconscious associations, not
yours.

I still say that the analytical processing of dream
associations makes anything possible, for what Healy,
Bronner, and Bowers said of Jones is even truer of
Freud. "In running through . . . [his work] on dream-
interpretation we find that recognition is required
of opposites, distortions, reversals, absurdities which
are distortions welcomed by resistance, transpositions,
twistings, modifications, transformations, references,
representatives, symbolizations, fusions, combinations,
allusions, hidden connections and motivations, contradictions, substitutions, displacements, reminiscences,
wishes—superficial as against deeper, expediences, con-
jurings up, inversions, repressions, elaborations,
interchanges."[58]

What subtlety! What inanity! The analytic interpretation of dreams is truly poker with everything
wild. Everything is anything, and the more farfetched
and forced, the better is the dream interpretation—to
the analyst, if not the patient.

Freud has said that the interpretation of dreams of
falling "when they occur in women, offers no difficulty, because they nearly always accept the symbolic
meaning of falling, which is a circumlocution for

* I think it would be cutting corners to say
Fungus—a noun, therefore—
Pronoun.

giving way to an erotic temptation."[59] Aside from being a bit of sophistry, this illustrates Freud's belief in the *play on words and their associations as a technique of dream interpretation.*

The fallacy of this principle could be demonstrated by going over the dreams of some of Freud's long-dead patients, but I think that it would be even more instructive to apply this technique (among others) to some of the very dreams that Freud himself dreamed. I shall give you Freud's interpretation of one of his own dreams, then I shall give you Fromm's interpretation of the same dream. I shall follow it with my own pseudo-analytical interpretation, and close with Velikovsky's curious interpretation of that very same dream. All the interpretations will be different, and if they are not plausible, at least they will be interesting. In any case, here are Freud's own dreams and the divergent interpretations for each.

Freud wrote that he had once dreamed he had "written a monograph on a certain plant. The book lies before me; I am just turning over a folded coloured plate. A *dried specimen* of the plant, as though from a *herbarium,* is bound up with every copy."[60] (Italics mine.)

Freud explains the particular form of the dream by saying that in the morning he had seen "in a bookseller's window, a volume entitled *The Genus Cyclamen,* apparently a monograph on this plant." Freud's further associations are as follows:

(1) "The *cyclamen* is my wife's favourite flower. I reproach myself for remembering so seldom to bring her flowers, as she would like me to do."[61]

(2) The *dried specimen* of the plant suggests:

(3) *Herbarium,* which in turn Freud associates with:
(4) *Crucifers* (plants with four-petaled flowers).

A few more associations lead Freud to *artichoke flowers* and the remark that, "My wife, more thoughtful than I, often brings this favourite flower of mine home from the market."[62] Freud thereafter goes on to other and more remote associations. To Freud, then, this dream simply illustrates "the material and sources of dreams," and that he is "much too absorbed" in his hobbies.

But Fromm has advanced another interpretation of this dream. To him Freud is reprimanding himself for showing a lack of consideration for his wife. Freud does not even mention this possibility—though he is often quite frank about his own dreams and his interpretations. Fromm writes of Freud, "In other words, the monograph about the cyclamen stirs up his feeling that he fails in that aspect of life which is symbolized by love and tenderness. All the other associations point in one direction, that of his ambition."[63]

Now I shall introduce a *third* and related interpretation of Freud's dream. What would Freud, according to analytic doctrine, have told a patient who dreamed of a *dried* specimen of plant *that reminded him of his wife?* Freud, without doubt, would have told the patient that he was no longer interested in his wife sexually. Freud's writings abound with flower dreams analogously interpreted.

More generally, Freud says, *"Blossoms and flowers* represent the female sexual organs. . . In this connection you will recollect that the blossoms are really the sexual organs of plants."[64] And again, "sexual flower-symbolism, which, of course, is very widespread, symbolizes the human sexual organs by flowers, the sexual organs of plants."[65] And dried flowers, of course . . .

The fourth, and most interesting interpretation of Freud's dream of the cyclamen, is provided by Velikovsky.[66] To him,

(1) Monograph would be the writings on *monotheism*
(2) Herbarium suggests *Hebrew,* and
(3) "To page through also means to turn the pages (*umschlagen*)," to *convert.*
(4) Crucifers suggest *crucifixes,* and
(5) Cyclamen contains the word *amen.*

Freud in this dream is obviously distressed at the thought of being a Jew and wants to become a Catholic—at least that is the meaning according to Freud's own technique of dream interpretation. Freud wrote about the fascination Moses always held for him: "How often have I mounted the steep steps of the unlovely Corso Cavour to the lonely place where the deserted church stands, and have essayed to support the angry scorn of the hero's glance! Sometimes I have crept cautiously out of the half-gloom of the interior as though I myself belonged to the mob upon whom his eye is turned—the mob which can hold fast no conviction, which has neither faith nor patience and which rejoices when it has regained its illusory idols."[67]

Velikovsky gives further reasons in support of his interpretation of Freud's dream, but to me his parallel interpretation of still another of Freud's dreams—a dream about Rome—will serve to prove how in analytic dream interpretation anything can always stand for anything else.

"In a third dream," says Freud, "I am at last in *Rome*. To my disappointment the scenery is anything but urban: it consists of a little stream of *black water,* on one side of which are *black rocks,* while on the other are *meadows* with *large white flowers.* . . ."[68] (All italics are mine.)

As for its interpretation, "It is obvious," says Freud, "that I am trying in vain to see in my dream a city which I have never seen in my waking life. . . . The white flowers point to Ravenna, which is known to me, and which once, for a time, replaced Rome as the capital of Italy. In the marshes around Ravenna we had found the most beautiful water-lilies in the midst of black pools of water; the dream makes them grow in the meadows . . . The black rock so close to the water vividly recalls the valley of the Tepl at Karlsbad. . . ." and more in the same vein.

Oh no, says Velikovsky. Freud is still disturbed at being a Jew and still wants to become a Catholic. For,

1. "Rome" stands for the *Roman Catholic Church.*
2. "Black water" is the water for *baptism.*
3. "Black rocks"—*Judaism,* the unhappy life of the Jews. On the other side of which are
4. "Meadows with large white flowers," i.e., *Christianity,* the happy life of those who are not persecuted.

Freud, says Velikovsky, is dreaming he is in "Rome." The baptismal water ("black water") separates Judaism ("black rocks") from the happy Christian "meadows with large white flowers."

I myself could give another, and equally impressive, pseudo-analytic interpretation of this dream. I could mechanically interpret the "little stream of black water, on one side of which are black rocks" as the female genitals, and I could also—but no. I think this is quite enough. Freud's dreams, in fact, *anyone's dreams,* can receive an almost infinite series of psychoanalytic interpretations. All of the interpretations can be made to interlock, indicating, to an analyst, accurate interpretation; but to everybody else, it is only hamburger from the psychoanalytic meat grinder.

Freud was once asked why " 'should one continue to use symbols in one's dreams when one is perfectly willing to think of the original object when awake?' In the course of his answer [to this very neat question] he said certain symbols were firmly established in the human mind and transmitted from generation to generation through heredity."[69]

Which leads to *my next objection to psychoanalytic dream interpretation, and that is that Freud advocated a doctrine of the archaic inheritance of symbols, which is without the slightest basis in fact whatever.* ". . . dreams," said Freud, "bring to light material which could not originate either from the dreamer's adult life or from his forgotten childhood. We are obliged to regard it as part of the *archaic heritage* which a child brings with him into the world, before any experience of his own, as a result of the experiences of his ancestors."[70] ". . . the archaic heritage of mankind includes not only dispositions, but also ideational contents, memory traces of the experiences of former generations."[71] "It seems to me . . . that symbolism, a mode of expression which has never been individually acquired, may claim to be regarded as a racial heritage."[72] In this connection, Freud symbolically interprets a dream that a patient of his had as a child. Says Freud, "It is naturally a very striking phenomenon that symbolism should already play a part in the dream of a child of four, but this is the rule rather than the exception. One may say that the dreamer has command of symbolism from the very first."[73]

Freud's contention that children inherit dream symbols, unreasonable as the statement may be, cannot be disproven any more than it can be proven. But we do know today that our social experiences determine our reactions to people and things. Consequently, certain similar experiences, in certain similar cultural backgrounds, can give people similar reactions to their environment. As soon as we look upon the individual as the child of the society in which he finds himself, we see quickly enough that there is no need to postulate inherited symbols of rivers and mountains, water and fruit, and all the rest of the Freudian heraldic devices. Sleeping—as well as waking—associations are dependent completely upon the individual's experiences, and upon the culture he has absorbed.

In the last book he ever wrote, Freud still preached the inheritance of dream symbols from our prehistoric ancestors.[74] He stuck to this belief, despite the decades of progress that psychology, sociology, and anthropology had made since he first uttered his opinion. I must say, however, that some analysts have discarded Freud's archaic inheritance theory, but they still keep the symbols derived from it!

Now I shall move on to still another fallacy that underlies psychoanalytic dream interpretation, and though this error can be explained in a few lines, it is of a particularly critical nature. *Freud almost completely ignored the activity of the higher levels of the mind.* Scholars have deciphered ancient inscriptions, poets have written poems, and complicated mathematical problems have been solved, all in dreams. But Freud had to stay away from this unconscious *intellectual* activity, for had he gone into it, he would have been in a dilemma. He would have had to show that unconscious dream thinking is essentially similar to conscious everyday thought. And conscious thinking is something we all are familiar with, and about which we accept no nonsense about castration and the Oedipus complex. Freud's entire theory would have been threatened if he had granted the far-reaching parallelisms between conscious and unconscious thinking.

The consequence is that Freud had to propound a colossal inaccuracy and say that "the psychic activity in dream-formation . . . is something altogether different, qualitatively, from waking thought, and cannot therefore be compared with it."[75] Psychoanalysis, of course, is based on elaborate distinctions between conscious and unconscious, and when those distinctions fade, psychoanalysis fades with it.

The emphasis that is placed upon dreams in analytic treatment *is quite dangerous to the patient's mental health*—and this forms the kernel of another criticism I must raise against analytic dream interpretation. The tremendous importance placed upon dreams by the Freudians takes the patient away from his immediate environment and increases his tendency to withdraw from reality. He starts to wonder what is "really" behind his actions, for he becomes convinced that his unconscious is constantly at work trying to trick him. The patient's doubts about himself (which brought him to analysis) begin to increase, and he starts to suggest more and more worry to himself. The fact that analysis is a matter of long duration tends to increase the possibility that this doubt and withdrawal may become a way of life.

To the analytic statement that this introspection is nothing but a transitory phase, my reply is that I do not doubt that the analysts would like this state of affairs to be transitory. Nevertheless, it must be realized that introspection and self-doubt are implicit in every single step of the analytic procedure, and it is even implicit in the *objective* of analytic therapy. For Freud stated the therapeutic aim of psychoanalysis to be the replacing of the unconscious by the conscious.[76] This brings to mind the story of the centipede who never had any trouble walking until one day he was asked which foot he moved forward first. The more he thought about it, the more he got confused and fell all over himself trying to get started. The unhappy centipede had replaced his unconscious by his conscious—and that is what the psychoanalysts would have us do. Once more we can see how right the analyst was who said that even if a patient were "normal at the beginning of the analysis, the analytic procedure would create a neurosis."[77]

Psychoanalysis, with the introspection of dream interpretation, gives no help in solving the problems of everyday life. When an analyst says that by analyzing dreams he is showing his patients the contents of their unconscious so they can better cope with everyday life, he is doing no such thing. What he is doing is giving his sick patients Freudian fictions, which they are in grave danger of permanently confusing with facts.

More than that, in therapy we get very little from dreams that we can't get from a study of everyday life. Selling[78] "questioned two hundred boys about their dreams during the first week after they had entered a reformatory. He found that eighty per cent of the boys dreamed about home, mostly in connection with normal household routines . . ." This makes sense, but what calls for comment is that the subject of home and normal household routines also "represented the commonest content of their wishful phantasy during waking hours." This illustrates the fact that we get very little from dreams that we can't get from a study of the individual's waking fantasies and general behavior. The only exception that I will make is to say that forgotten childhood experiences may surge to the forefront in dreams, but the increasing belief in psychotherapy is that the recapture of memories of the past is of no importance in making an individual feel better today.

Incidentally, throughout this chapter we have been taking for granted that although the analysts are in error in interpreting dreams, the patients at least are correct in reporting them. I should now like to examine this assumption.

We have all had the experience of completely forgetting the fact that we had dreamed the night before, and suddenly recalling the dream later the next day. If a dream can be forgotten in its entirety, surely it can be forgotten in part. This, of course, means that an analyst may often get an incomplete and distorted picture of the patient's dream. On the basis of Freud's own argument, certain repressions operate to mask portions of childhood remembrances, and similar repressions operate in an individual's recollection of his dreams.

And what, I might ask, of the reverse possibility, i.e., that the patient adds subtly erroneous details to his dreams as he tries to recall them? According to Freud's own assumptions *all* the details in a dream have significance. Without going into any further considerations, I think it fair to say that from Freud's point of view, or from any other, there can be no question that the very dreams that are presented to a psychoanalyst are highly suspect as being, in many important details, as inaccurate as the seduction fantasies that Freud used to find in his patients.

Well, the reader may say, to make sure we remember our dreams accurately, why not write them down immediately on awakening? This would seem reasonable, at least if one were interested in remembering one's dreams. But Freud opposed such a procedure, and with his completely circular argument:

". . . we often find that a patient may try to combat the forgetting of his dreams by writing them down immediately after he wakes up. We may as well tell him that it is useless to do so, because the resistance from which he may have preserved the text of the dream will then transfer itself to the associations and render the manifest dream inaccessible for interpretation. This being the case, we need not be surprised if a further increase of the resistance suppresses the associations altogether, and thus frustrates the interpretation of the dream entirely."[79]

Rather than say that Freud's position is nonsense on the face of it, which is my first inclination, I shall force myself to take it seriously and go over it. Assuming, solely for the sake of argument, that there are such things as "resistances" and "manifest dream contents," what Freud was saying in essence was this:

> It is futile to write down one's dreams on awakening, because the resistances from which one may have preserved the manifest text of the dream will transfer themselves to the associations of the dream.

Is the alternative any better? Certainly carrying a highly perishable dream around in one's head, subject to all of the vagaries of memory and the distractions of the day, makes the accuracy of such a remembered dream highly problematic. In that event, its "manifest content" would surely fade, and it is from this "manifest content" that associations are developed. Just what did Freud have against writing down one's dreams anyway, for his argument against it is weak, even according to his own theories? I do not know why Freud was opposed to patients' writing down their dreams. I can only guess. And my guess is that a solid piece of paper, with a dream accurately written down on it, is too narrow and confining a take-off point for the broad wings of unrestrained and unverifiable fancy on which psychoanalytic dream interpretation depends.

There is just one more point I want to make about the psychoanalytic interpretation of dreams, and then we shall be done with it. *Analytic dream interpreta-*

*tion is permeated, corrupted, distorted, and made
meaningless by suggestion.*

Freud was aware of this serious possibility, and here
is how he answered it. "The question of the value to
be assigned to dreams is intimately related to the
other question of their susceptibility to influence from
'suggestion' by the physician. Analysts may at first be
alarmed at the mention of this possibility. But on
further reflection this alarm will give place to the
realization that the influencing of the patient's dreams
is no more a blunder on the part of the analyst or dis-
grace to him than the guiding of the patient's conscious thoughts."[80]

Freud develops further his admission that the patient's dreams are influenced by the analytic procedure.

"The fact that the manifest content of dreams is influenced by the analytic treatment stands in no need
of proof. It follows from our knowledge that dreams
are dependent upon waking life and work over material derived from it. Occurrences during analytic
treatment are of course among the impressions of
waking life and soon become some of the most powerful of these. So it is not to be wondered at that patients
should dream of things which the analyst has discussed
with them and of which he has aroused expectations
in them."[81]

This is definite enough—but wait, says Freud. "We
can often influence what a man shall dream *about,* but
never *what* he will dream; for the mechanism of the
dream-work and the unconscious dream-wish are inaccessible to external influence of any sort."[82]

Freud did not see the far-reaching implications of

these admissions. Some lines back he granted that the analyst guided a "patient's conscious thoughts." By this he could not possibly have meant "the patient's [*manifest*] conscious thoughts," else what point would there be in any analytic guidance at all? The object of analytic guidance is to change the emotions *behind* the conscious thoughts. At the same time Freud would have us believe that although the analytic procedure affects the patient's waking feelings, it nevertheless has no effect on the feelings of the sleeping patient— which is most illogical—i.e., "the mechanism of the dream-work and the unconscious dream-wish are inaccessible to external influence of any sort." And to compound the illogic even more, one of the key signs of improvement alleged in psychoanalytic therapy *is* a change in the "hidden" meanings of the patient's dreams, and the analysts, of course, believe that these changes stem from the analytic procedure.

The unsoundness of Freud's denial of analytic influence on the "hidden" meaning of dreams, can be shown in another way. Freud says, "there must be some motive power, some unconscious force, which is better able to lend support to the purposes of analysis during the *state of sleep* than at other times. What is here in question cannot well be any factor other than the patient's compliance towards the analyst which is derived from his parental complex—in other words, the positive portion of what we call the transference; and in fact, in many dreams which recall what has been forgotten and repressed, *it is impossible to discover any other unconscious wish to which the motive force for the formation of the dream can be attributed.*"[83] (Italics mine.)

This, of course, is clear admission that a patient in the grip of the analytic transference *does* have the "unconscious wish" in his dream seriously influenced.

Let me give the reader a compass bearing as we wander through the psychoanalytic maze. The point I am making is that contrary to Freud's denials, analytic dream interpretation is permeated, corrupted, distorted, and made meaningless by suggestion. I think that my dissection of Freud's disclaimers has already established my point, but I have even more evidence.

Freud said on another occasion,

> It looks as though the patient had had the amiability to reproduce for us in dream-form exactly what we had been "suggesting" to him immediately beforehand in the treatment. The more experienced analyst . . . recognizes that [such dreams] . . . are only to be observed under certain conditions brought about under the influence of the treatment. The great majority of the dreams forge ahead of the analysis, so that, *after subtraction of all that in them which is already known and understood,* there still remains a more or less clear indication of something hitherto deeply hidden.[84] (Italics mine.)

Notice what Freud does in this quotation. He starts by saying that "it looks as though the patient had the amiability to reproduce for us in dream-form exactly what we had been 'suggesting' to him . . ." Obviously, Freud does not think that the dreams of the patient are a result of any suggestion. That's clear enough.

Freud then proceeds to weaken his contention. "The more experienced analyst . . . recognizes that [such dreams] . . . are only to be observed under certain conditions brought about under the influence of the treatment." "The influence of the treatment," of course, includes the suggestive influence of the "transference."

Freud then concludes that "after subtraction of all that . . . is already known and understood" about the dreams, "there still remains a more or less clear indication of something hitherto deeply hidden." In short, to get the "deeply hidden" there has to be some "subtraction" from the dream. But the very nature of the analytic procedure makes it absolutely impossible to differentiate between the "subtraction of all that . . . is already known and understood," and all that has already been implanted by the analytic processing.

In fact, Freud even admitted that an analyst can subtract the patient's dreams *completely*. "One must generally guard against displaying special interest in the meaning of dreams . . . otherwise there is a danger of resistance being directed against the production of dreams and a risk of bringing about a cessation of them."[85] Such counsel to analysts, of course, is completely unrealistic, for 99 per cent of their patients over the last 50 years have known of the overwhelming importance that psychoanalysts attach to dreams. At any rate, says Freud, "The more the patient has learnt of the method of dream-interpretation the more obscure do his later dreams become, as a rule. All the acquired knowledge about dreams serves also as a warning to the dream-work."[86]

It was all put in a nutshell by a woman I treated. "I dreamed Freudian dreams for Dr. X, Jungian dreams for Dr. Y, and Adlerian dreams for Dr. Z."

For our purposes, all we need remember is that psychoanalytic dream interpretation is really the psychoanalytic interpretation of the results of psychoanalytic suggestion. It is without any serious or useful significance. In fact, we may say it is not even the interpretation of dreams at all. It is the psychoanalytic *interpolation* of dreams—the *interpolation* of meanings, the *interpolation* of distortions, the *interpolation* of suggestions. It is not the dreamer dreaming. It is the psychoanalyst dreaming for the dreamer.

5

PSYCHOANALYTIC
NORMALITY

*The governing laws of logic have no sway in the
unconscious; it might be called the Kingdom
of the Illogical.*[1]

—SIGMUND FREUD

ALTHOUGH that was how Freud referred to the
psychoanalytic interpretation of dreams, he might
well have been describing his ridiculous conception
of mental normality. For we must remember, after all,
that analytic treatment aims at making people normal.
In Freud's words, "Let us assume that what analysis
achieves for neurotics is only what normal people accomplish for themselves without its help."[2] Fair
enough. Besides, said Freud, "Our object will be not
to rub off all the corners of the human character so as
to produce 'normality' according to schedule, nor yet
to demand that the person who has been 'thoroughly
analysed' shall never again feel the stirrings of passions
in himself or become involved in any internal conflict."[3] Again fair enough.

But a fundamental fallacy underlies the therapeutic objectives of psychoanalysis. To Freud and his successors, "The therapeutic effect of analysis depends on the making conscious what is, in the widest sense, repressed within the id."[4] Or as Kubie put it, "Human behavior is normal precisely to the degree to which it is determined by conscious forces, and neurotic insofar as it is determined by unconscious forces."[5]

This is in direct contradiction to two points. First, it contradicts Freud's belief that ". . . normality developed as the result of repression of certain component-instincts and components of the infantile disposition . . ."[6] And secondly, it contradicts the fact that the so-called normal individual is happiest to the extent that his UNconscious processes govern his life. When we are least self-conscious, when we are least aware of what we are doing, only then do we feel at our best. This is well illustrated by the person who needs a drink or two in order to permit his UNconscious processes to dominate him.

I hold no particular brief for alcohol (or the barbiturates) as a method of giving the individual a chemical feeling of freedom, but I think it important to point out that happy states are associated with *freedom* of expression. "Therapy, in Freud's view then [I am quoting Mullahy], effects not primarily a liberation of individuality by the release of creative potentialities for life experiences, but a restoration of our ability to control our crude drives."[7]

The only possible defense that the analysts could introduce at this point would be to make one of their meaningless distinctions. In this case they would contend that the unconscious forces to which they are opposed are the *repressed* experiences in the patient's childhood. They are not opposed to the patient's *un*-repressed experiences. This differentiation is untenable, for we know that to take any well-adjusted individual, and to subject him to the psychoanalytic process of making him conscious of even his *emotionally fortunate* early experiences, would have the usual result. The once-happy patient would become quite conscious of his mental processes—and become introspective and self-analytical. He would, in fact, become neurotic—and all by achieving the sworn objective of psychoanalysis!

According to the psychoanalysts, boys grow into normality when they give up their Oedipus complex. Said Freud, "At a certain moment the child comes to understand that an attempt to remove his father as a rival would be punished by him with castration. So from fear of castration, that is, in the interests of preserving his masculinity, he gives up his wish to possess his mother and get rid of his father. . . . We believe that what we have here been describing are the *normal processes, the normal fate* of the so-called 'Oedipus complex' . . ."[8] (Italics mine.) The key point, then, in this achievement of normality is that "the boy's Oedipus complex, in which he desires his mother, and wants to get rid of his father as a rival, develops naturally . . . The threat of castration, however, forces him to give up this attitude. Under the influence of the danger of losing his penis, he abandons his Oedipus-complex . . ."[9] To the analysts the Oedipus complex disappears normally because the boy believes that his father has said, "You miserable little rascal. You'd better stay away from my wife (i.e., your mother) or I'll castrate you." Freud does not tell us why it takes so long for a boy to realize that his father feels like a jealous bull, and that all poachers on his father's sexual property will receive cruel and unusual punishment. The resolution of the Oedipus complex by castration fear is ridiculous—but it is no more ridiculous than the Oedipus complex itself.

Freud's thoughts about the "normal" disappearance of the Oedipus complex suffer from a critical inconsistency in logic. If we grant that the disappearance of the Oedipus complex is necessary to the attainment of normality, and if we grant that the disappearance of the Oedipus complex is achieved through castration fear, does it not appear as if normality is acquired as a result of fear and repression exerted upon the boy? And is not the achievement of mental health *by repression* in flagrant contradiction of the most elementary Freudian doctrines?

It certainly is, and Freud admitted it. "I see no reason to deny the name of 'repression' to the ego's turning from the Oedipus-complex . . ."[10] But repression, of course, is wicked, so Freud modified this by saying, "But the process described is more than a repression; when carried out in the ideal way it is equivalent to a destruction and abrogation of the complex."[11] It "is repressed and in the most normal cases entirely destroyed."[12] What Freud is saying is that sometimes repression is not repression, but is annihilation of the content repressed. This, of course, contradicts everything else Freud ever said.

Even those most sympathetic to Freud find the contradictions in the Oedipus complex somewhat confusing. Says the *Psychiatric Dictionary* of the passing of the Oedipus complex, "The fate of the Oedipus complex is not yet clearly understood."[13] I think we can talk with certainty of the fate of the Oedipus complex. The fate of the Oedipus complex will be the fate of alchemy, and phrenology, and palmistry. The fate of the Oedipus complex will be oblivion. It is almost sad to see Freud writing, in his last book, "I venture to assert that if psychoanalysis could boast of no other achievement than the discovery of the repressed Oedipus complex, that alone would give it a claim to be counted among the precious new acquisitions of mankind."[14]

When the Oedipus complex is repressed into annihilation (ignoring Freud's contradictions for the moment), then, says Freud, "It is not a great step to assume that here we have come upon the borderland between normal and pathological which is never very sharply defined."[15] Here, loitering at the border between normality and abnormality we meet our old friend Oedipus. You see, sometimes Oedipus is not repressed quite appropriately, and then that incomplete repression "persists unconsciously in the *id*, and will express itself later on in some pathogenic effect."[16]

What with the Oedipus complex being so important, what with its repression determining normality or abnormality, and what with castration fear sometimes the cause of neurosis and sometimes the cause of mental health, how can the psychoanalytic distinction between normality and abnormality be anything except meaningless? Said Freud, ". . . there is scarcely any condition generally recognized as normal in which it would not be possible to demonstrate neurotic traits."[17] ". . . psychoanalysis recognizes no essential distinction, but only quantitative differences, between the psychic life of the normal person and that of the neurotic . . ."[18] "[The] distinction, [between what is psychologically normal and abnormal] in spite of its practical importance, possesses only a conventional value."[19]

In the Freudian never-never land there is no difference between imitation and genuine. There, Freud says, "every normal person is only approximately normal: his ego resembles that of the psychotic in one point or another, in a greater or lesser degree."[20] Normal is abnormal, and abnormal is normal. And any distinctions between them? These depend on the amount of repression of the Oedipus complex, or on vague statements about the relationships among id, ego, and super-ego—unless the difference between normal and abnormal is being described in hydraulic analogies about diverting primitive impulses into culturally acceptable channels (which most neurotics do anyway, and still remain unhappy).

The fact is that psychoanalysis has not devoted a great deal of attention to a study of the normal personality.[21] And when it has, it has made "discoveries" that make us wonder whether to laugh or commit mayhem.

Said Freud, as an infant "sinks asleep at the breast, utterly satisfied, it bears a look of perfect content which will come back again later in life after the experience of the sexual orgasm."[22] "Like the crying of a child after birth, singing in the bath means the wish to go back, the unconscious sexual longing for the mother."[23]

The "condition of being in love in ordinary life

outside analysis is also more like abnormal than normal mental phenomena."[24] "In no normal person does the normal sexual aim lack some designable perverse element."[25] "Parental love, which is so touching and at bottom so childish, is nothing but parental narcissism born again."[26] "It might be said that we owe the fairest flowers of our love-life to the reaction against the hostile impulse [i.e., unconscious death-wishes in regard to loved ones] which we divine in our breasts."[27]

As for friendship, said Freud, "In the light of psychoanalysis we are accustomed to regard social feeling as a sublimation [that is, deflection from the sexual aim] of homosexual attitudes towards objects."[28] And more broadly, "We have to conclude that *all the feelings of sympathy, friendship, trust and so forth which we expend in life are genetically connected with sexuality and have developed out of purely sexual desires by an enfeebling of their sexual aim, however pure and non-sensual they may appear* in the forms they take on to our conscious self-perception. To begin with we know none but sexual objects; *psycho-analysis shows us that those persons whom in real life we merely respect or are fond of may be sexual objects to us in our unconscious minds still.*"[29] (Italics mine.)

Freud was as wrong about normality as he was about abnormality. He brought the same erroneous obscenities to *all* aspects of human behavior.

"All disputes about the psychogenesis of the neuroses," Freud once said, "must eventually be decided on the field of the neuroses of childhood. Careful dissection of a neurosis in early childhood puts an end to all misapprehensions about the aetiology of the neuroses and to all doubts about the part played by the *sexual impulses* in them."[30] (Italics mine.)

If true, this is very interesting, but, said Freud, "Investigation into the mental life of normal persons . . . yielded the unexpected discovery that their infantile history in regard to sexual matters was not necessarily different in essentials from that of the neurotic . . ."[31] If you can't find the critical difference between two groups, as called for by a theory, why not throw out the theory? No. Freud simply broadened his theory, to make the original critical difference no longer critical. Now, since everybody would be included, it would look like a scientific discovery.

"Since we came to see more clearly we have been tempted to say that childhood neurosis is not the exception but the rule; it is as though it were unavoidable in the passage from the infantile disposition to conformity with the culture achieved by society. In most cases, these neurotic spells of early years are overcome spontaneously; it may be that their traces are usually left in those of *average mental health*."[32] (Italics mine.) Freud, we will note, here blames neurosis on societal repression, rather than on individual sexual biography. But since in similar cultures there are the same essential repressions, and since Freud grants that the "infantile history [of normal persons] in regard to sexual matters [is] not necessarily different in essentials from that of the neurotic . . ."[33] Freud has not explained a single solitary thing.

The importance of childhood in the determination of character has had a long and honorable history, both before Freud and after him. What Freud did was

to introduce a preposterous sexuality into this childhood and thus obstruct the development of a sound
science of child psychology. Freud writes, "What poets
and students of human nature had always asserted
turned out to be true: the impressions of that remote
period of life, though they were for the most part
buried in amnesia, left ineradicable traces upon the
individual's growth and in particular laid the founda-
tions of any nervous disorder that was to follow. But
since these experiences of childhood were always concerned with sexual excitations and the reaction against
them, I found myself faced by the fact of infantile
sexuality—once again a novelty and a contradiction of
one of the strongest of human prejudices."[34]

Now, parents and teachers and nurses, and everybody else who deals with children, have known for
centuries that infants have sexuality. The only question that arises is whether infantile sexuality is the
preposterous sexuality of the analysts, or whether it is
not. I somehow don't think that it is true that, as
Freud said, "If the child has any sexual life at all, it
can only be of a perverse nature."[35] Or that, "With
boys the wish to beget a child from their mother is
never absent, with girls the wish to have a child by
their father is equally constant . . ."[36]

Psychoanalytic apologists, in an effort to make
Freudian sexuality more plausible, have said, "You
know, Freud neither invented nor discovered the
sexual life of the child. He only studied it." Not at all.
He misrepresented it. Pitirim Sorokin put it charitably. "What is sound in Freudianism is very old, what
is new, very doubtful."

Some of Freud's thoughts about childhood have a phantasmagoric quality. "The women patients characterized by a strong attachment to the mother, in whom I have been able to study the pre-Oedipus phase, have all told me that when their mother gave them enemas or rectal douches they used to offer the strongest possible resistance and react with fear and screams of rage. This is probably very usual or even universal with children. I only came to understand the reasons for this specially passionate struggle through a remark by Ruth Mack Brunswick, who was studying these problems at the same time as I was. She said that she would compare the outbreak of fury after an enema with the orgasm following on genital excitation. The accompanying anxiety should be construed as a transformation of the desire for aggression which had been stirred up. I believe that this is actually the case . . ."[37]

Here is something even more preposterous. "Since the column of faeces stimulates the erotogenic mucous membrane of the intestine, it plays the part of an active organ in regard to it; it behaves just as the penis does to the vaginal mucous membrane, and acts as it were as its precursor during the cloacal epoch. The handing over of faeces for the sake of (out of love for) some one else becomes a prototype of castration; it is the first occasion upon which an individual gives up a piece of his own body . . . in order to gain the favour of some other person whom he loves. So that a person's love of his own penis, which is in other respects narcissistic, is not without an element of anal erotism. 'Faeces,' 'child,' and 'penis' thus form a unity, an unconscious concept . . ."[38]

Freud sees a key to the unconscious mind in all this. "It is impossible to have any understanding of people's phantasies, or of associations which occur under the influence of the unconscious, or of the language of symptoms, if one does not know about these deep-lying connections. On this level, faeces-money-gift-child-penis are taken as having the same meaning, and can be represented by the same symbols."[39]

Now we must not laugh, for Freud's successors have elevated these cogitations into a philosophy of child care, and an entire *Weltanschauung*. As Orlansky says, in a devastating article, "The *'oral-anal'* view of personality and culture, as it may be called, holds that the infant's early experiences in feeding and toilet training determine *his adult character, and that this character, in turn, determines the nature of his culture,* since most adults in any culture have received similar training during childhood. On the basis of this theory, an increasing number of pediatricians have been instructing mothers in methods of infant care, and some anthropologists have been conducting investigations of foreign cultures.

"The tenor of these investigations may, perhaps, be suggested by an earlier study—Geoffrey Gorer's analysis of Japanese culture. It attributes the 'overwhelming brutality and sadism of the Japanese at war,' their type of ethics, their famous Tea Ceremony, and their landscape gardening to the early bowel training of Japanese infants. Gorer has also analyzed the 'national character' of Andean Indians, Russians, Burmese, and Americans in terms of their mechanisms of infant rearing—how long and how often infants are breast-fed, when toilet training is instituted, and whether or not the infant is swaddled or cradled after birth. Some social scientists, following in his footsteps, seem engaged in the creation of a new science of history in which war, Nazism, Stalinism, free enterprise, and other manifestations of 'national character' are explained by such infant disciplines."[40] (Italics mine.)

My own comments on these psychoanalytic digressions will have to wait for some other occasion. Here I shall endeavor to confine myself to Freud's thoughts on children—from which thoughts were developed the current theories about the relationship of toilet training to world peace. "The [child's] interest," says Freud, "which has hitherto been attached to excrement is carried over on to other objects—for instance, from faeces on to money, which is late in acquiring significance for children."[41] "The child has no knowledge of money other than that received as a gift, no idea of money earned or belonging to it, inherited. Since its faeces constitute its first gift, the child easily transfers interest from this substance to the new one that meets it as the most valuable form of gift in life. . . . Thus the interest in faeces is carried on partly as interest in money [and], partly as a wish for a child . . ."[42]

And that, said Freud, is how a child can become an *anal personality*—one of those people who manifest "a regular combination of the three following peculiarities: they are exceptionally *orderly, parsimonious,* and *obstinate.*"[43] And eight years later Freud added "avarice, pedantry and stubbornness" to the personality qualities that draw "powerful contributions" from anal-erotic sources.[44] According to the psychoanalysts, therefore, stamp collecting, antique collecting, an interest in business, a desire to take care of one's clothes and possessions, any of the aspects of thrift, saving little leftovers in the refrigerator for a midnight snack, all these are aspects of the anal personality. Incidentally, according to Freud, "bodily cleanliness and reliability and conscientiousness in the performance of petty duties"[45] are also related to the anal personality.

Freud worried the topic thoroughly. "It is as well . . . [he said] to bear in mind Abraham's reminder that embryologically the anus corresponds to the primitive mouth, which has moved down to the end of the bowel . . . But the interest in the penis has, besides an anal-erotic basis, a perhaps even more powerful root in oral erotism; for in accordance with the situation of sucking, the penis derives a great deal from the nipple of the mother's breast."[46]

And this gives us some of the background for the Freudian concept of the *oral personality*. People who smoke, or like liquids or sweets, or bite their nails, manifest signs of this oral personality.[47] This form of personality is an aspect of what Freud called "the earliest recognizable sexual organization [i.e.,] the so-called 'cannibalistic' or 'oral' phase."[48] The "gratified oral type," says Glover, "tends to be optimistic and generous, [and] a frustrated oral type impatient, envious, grudging and easily depressed . . ."[49] Without doubt, Freud could be classified as a frustrated oral type, but it is neither fair nor relevant to discuss it here, so I will pass over it and refer the interested reader to other sources.[50]

The ghosts of Freud's moldy speculations on oral

and anal eroticism, the Oedipus complex, castration fear, and all the rest, still haunt much of the contemporary writing on child care. Here is a fairly typical example, taken from a magazine which a good number of intelligent mothers read. What would happen to children if they were brought up by parents who believed that "Although the boy loves his father, he feels hostility toward him; and he fears that in return the father will become angry and try to destroy his masculinity ... The conflicts during the Oedipal struggle give rise to anxieties that are reflected in the child's dreams and in his play. Fears and nightmares are again frequent. The little boy's dreams give evidence of the source of his anxiety. Around this time they are mainly concerned with bodily harm inflicted on him by terrifying figures—animal and human—who represent the parent most dangerous to him, the father. These anxious feelings are often displaced from the genital itself, and the little boy may show a preoccupation with broken or lost things or intense anxiety about minor injuries like cuts or even about getting his hair cut or going to the toilet. .... At this time the little girl's wish to be a boy comes from her feeling that her mother would love her more if she were. She interprets the lack of the male organ, which to her means loss of love, as a punishment for her aggressive wishes."[51]

I can't believe that parents who bring up children according to these principles would be completely satisfied with the outcome.

Freud once said, "The view [i.e., the psychoanalytic view] that the majority of our children pass through a neurotic phase in the course of their development automatically raises a hygienic question. It may be asked whether it would not be advantageous to come to the aid of a child with analysis *even where there is no sign of a disturbance,* as a precautionary measure in the interests of its health, just as nowadays one inoculates healthy children against diphtheria, without waiting for them to fall ill of the disease. . . . [The] greater number of our contemporaries would regard the mere idea as nothing short of criminal, and, when one considers the attitude of most parents towards analysis, one must, as yet, give up any hope of its realisation."[52] (Italics mine.)

What other attitude, besides horror, did Freud expect parents to have about "prophylactic" analysis anyway? After all, most parents do love their children and would prefer not to risk their health and happiness in the psychoanalytic swamps.

6

ANALYSIS TERMINABLE
AND INTERMINABLE

*You are perhaps aware that I have never been
a therapeutic enthusiast ... Every analyst ought
periodically himself to enter analysis once more,
at intervals of, say, five years, and without any
feeling of shame in so doing. So not only the
patient's analysis but that of the analyst himself
has ceased to be a terminable and become an
interminable task.[1]*

—SIGMUND FREUD

As Freud acknowledged, analysis is often an "interminable task," but for different reasons with different patients. Nevertheless, one reason, I think, that always applies, is simply that psychoanalysis is so incredibly unsound.

"The theories of resistance and of repression, of the unconscious," said Freud, "of the aetiological significance of sexual life and of the importance of infantile experiences—these form the principal constituents of the theoretical structure of psycho-analysis."[2] And

108

those, indeed, are the very theories that have been occupying us time and again, for the same themes recur with dreary regularity in any discussion of psychoanalysis. However, Freud's theories of *resistance* and *repression* still have a few unexplored aspects for us, and it is to those aspects that we shall now direct our attention.

Freud gave a broad definition of *resistance*. "We call *all the forces* which oppose the work of cure the patient's 'resistances.' "[3] (Italics mine.) That seems to cover everything. "The patient," said Freud, "does want to get well, but also he does not want to."[4] Said Freud, "you [will discover that you] have been deceived in your patient, that you cannot count at all on his co-operation and compliance, that he is ready to put every possible obstacle in the way of your joint task; in a word, that he does not want to become well at all . . . [This is] the actual truth—not the whole truth, but a noteworthy part of it."[5]

If the psychoanalysts looked upon people's neurotic difficulties as problems in habit formation, they would soon become aware that every habit has a habitual tendency to be habitual. Then they could do without their locust cloud of concepts and would not have to believe that for the purpose of resistance patients can take refuge in sudden silence or prolonged silence or even falling asleep on the analyst's couch. Nor would they believe that extreme fluency in giving free associations can be a sign of resistance, just as well as extreme hesitancy in giving free associations. For that matter, they say, patients can express resistance by aggravating old symptoms or by picking up new ones.[6] Or by *taking advantage* of the transference (Freud says the transference is "pre-eminently suitable as a weapon of resistance"[7]), or by *fighting* the transference. Why, says one English disciple of Freud, even expressing a wish for cure may be a disguised expression of an unconscious fantasy and serve the purpose of a resistance,[8] while another one says that repudiating the analyst's interpretations can be a sign of resistance. We can complete the fantasy of resistance with Freud's assertion that "there really *is* a resistance to the discovery of resistances . . ."[9]

Now all this, amusing as it may sound, is deadly serious analytic theory, applied in the treatment of unhappy people. Slowly, and almost silently, a web of frightening perplexity is spun around the patient. He *says* he wants to get well, but he doesn't, *really*. He has an unconscious desire to retain his neurosis. He is in a very bad way. Almost everything he does has a hidden meaning and shows his *resistance* to cure.

"The fight against all these resistances is the main work in the treatment," said Freud.[10] "It is one of the tasks of psycho-analysis to lift the veil of amnesia which shrouds the earliest years of childhood and to bring the expressions of infantile sexual life which are hidden behind it into conscious memory."[11] "The amount of effort required of the physician [i.e., the psychoanalyst]," said Freud, "varied in different cases; it increased in direct proportion to the difficulty of what had to be remembered. The expenditure of force on the part of the physician was evidently the measure of a *resistance* on the part of the patient. It was only necessary to translate into words what I myself had observed, and I was in possession of the theory of *repression*."[12]

Repression, then, is the cause of resistance. In fact, says Freud, "The doctrine of repression is the foundation-stone on which the whole structure of psychoanalysis rests."[13] But we mustn't take too seriously Freud's talk of repression as "the foundation-stone" of psychoanalysis. The Oedipus complex is just as much of a foundation-stone, and so is the castration complex. And Freud's division of mental activity into Eros and Thanatos certainly merits being called "the foundation-stone" of psychoanalysis. Although Freud once described *resistance* (not repression) as "one of the cornerstones" of his theory,[14] a cornerstone is certainly not the same as "the foundation-stone," but I shall not make any fastidious distinctions. I shall content myself with saying that psychoanalytic theory, with its foundation-stones and cornerstones, brings to mind the ancient druid ruins at Stonehenge. Once people worshiped there, but now the great stones have tumbled down and are only an attraction for tourists.

But we have been talking about *repression,* Freud's "foundation-stone." "[The] essence of repression," he said, "lies simply in the function of rejecting and keeping something out of consciousness."[15] And that is how the trouble starts. To the psychoanalysts a neurosis occurs only as a result of *repression.* It is the pushing down of painful memories into the unconscious, the *repression* of early experiences, that causes neurosis. "Decisive repressions all occur in early childhood."[16] If that's the case, why not lift the repressions? Why not free the genie from the bottle? And that's just what Freud did—but to no avail.

"In the early days of analytic technique . . . ," he wrote, "we . . . set a high value on the patient's knowledge of that which had been forgotten. . . . We accounted it specially fortunate if it were possible to obtain information of the forgotten traumas of childhood from external sources, from parents or nurses, for instance, or from the seducer himself, as occurred occasionally; and we hastened to convey the information and proofs of its correctness to the patient, in the certain expectation of bringing the neurosis and the treatment to a rapid end by this means. It was a bitter disappointment when the expected success was not forthcoming. How could it happen that the patient, who now had the knowledge of his traumatic experience, still behaved in spite of it as if he knew no more than before? Not even would the recollection of the repressed trauma come to mind after it had been told and described to him."[17]

From this Freud did not draw the obvious conclusion, to wit, that his concepts of resistance and repression were certainly nonsense in practice—and almost certainly nonsense in theory. Instead, Freud decided that, though "communicating to the patient's consciousness information about what is repressed . . . does not produce the hoped-for result of abolishing the symptoms . . . it has other consequences. It first arouses resistances, but when these are overcome [by transference and by explanation[18]] it sets a mental process in action, in the course of which the desired influence upon the unconscious memory is eventually effected."[19]

Freud is saying that efforts to abolish repressions and resistances result in the arousal of *new* resistances. And when these *new* resistances are overcome—"the desired influence upon the unconscious memory is eventually effected." It was Dr. Johnson who said, "My dear Madam, nonsense can only be defended by nonsense." I shall later show, *in Freud's own words*, that my interpretation of this passage is quite correct, and that it is the objective of psychoanalysis to give patients a *new* neurosis, and then to attempt to cure *that*.

The psychoanalysts have become quite disillusioned about recapturing memories as a method of treatment. Finding out on which side of which street a patient broke his leg is quite different from giving him antibiotics and setting his leg in splints. It has taken the analysts a long time to discover this. Nevertheless, their entire theoretical and therapeutic system is still permeated by the implications of Freud's original error in which he considered the objective of therapy to be the removal of repressions and resistances.

Freud carried his thinking about forgetting and repression to such lengths as to say that ". . . forgetting in all cases is proved to be founded on a motive of displeasure."[20] We forget what we want to forget. The fact is that the neurotic individual is almost invariably a woolgatherer, and he often forgets things he would most definitely like to remember. If we were to believe the analysts, persons forget gloves at a boring movie because they have an unconscious desire to return to it. We forget, say the analysts, in order to punish ourselves, and in order to obey the pressure of the super-ego. "The forgotten material," says Freud, "is not extinguished, only 'repressed.' "[21]

Besides repression and resistance, the psychoanalysts use such terms as *projection, identification, rationalization, sublimation,* and *displacement.* The only useful term in the lot is "rationalization"—and that dates from the middle of the nineteenth century. Of "sublimation," i.e., the analytic belief that infantile sex drives are sometimes not repressed but take on adult and seemingly nonsexual forms, Sears has said, succinctly, "The empirical evidence is sharply against the theory."[22]

Since Freud's Oedipus complexes, castration fears, cannibalistic desires, and murderous impulses have become increasingly ridiculous to most persons, there has developed a tendency among analysts to drop these terms with their patients. Now, rather than speak of repression of *castration* fear, sublimation of *sexuality,* and projection of *Oedipus desires,* they say that Freud spoke of repression, sublimation, projection, and all the rest. We can recognize the same principle here that was involved in analysts' saying that, after all, Freud *did* point out the role of the unconscious— whereas what Freud did was to *sexualize* the unconscious, an entirely different matter.

It is, of course, possible to talk of repression, sublimation, and all the rest of the Freudian fancies, but we must ask ourselves:

> —repression of what?
> —sublimation of what?
> —projection of what?

And then we see that the materials being chopped, broiled, fried, baked, and barbecued are the same old Oedipus complexes, libidinous urges, castration complexes, penis envy, and cannibalistic desires.

Although it is philosophically possible to differentiate between processes and the things being processed, it is not possible to do so in the case of psychoanalysis. For in psychoanalysis, repression and what is repressed (as an example) are Siamese twins with a single circulation, and to separate one from the other is to split apart the entire theoretical structure of psychoanalysis. Besides, to detach psychoanalytic processes from the psychoanalytic "things" being processed is to leave the processes suspended in thin air—with no relation to even the fictional things that Freud wrote about. This separation of analytic processes from analytic "things" is scientifically untenable—and even more untenable when the processes themselves are as fictitious as the things being processed.

Psychoanalysts, however well-meaning, who retain the Freudian mechanisms in their thinking—whether or not they mention those concepts to their patients— are not being fair, either to their patients or to their own desire to advance psychotherapy. Psychoanalysis bulges with terms and pat verbal formulae which look like answers but are not, and create the illusion of explanation and treatment where there is none. Anything that adds to the confusion is to be avoided.

As Sears said, ". . . where experimentation has gone forward with little attention to the specific forms of psychoanalytic theories it has made important strides. Instrumental act *fixation* and *regression* are examples in point; virtually none of the work on habit strength was instigated by analytic concepts. To a slightly lesser extent this appears to have been true of *substitution* as well. It is a pure happenstance that habit strength is closely related to *fixation*. . . . But the studies of *aggression, displacement, repression,* and *projection* serve no more than to give crude confirmation of phenomena that do not require it."[23] (Italics mine.)

The best comment about the psychoanalytic approach to problems was made in a somewhat different connection by William James many years ago. Said he, "It takes, in short, what Berkeley calls a mind debauched by learning to carry [on] the process of making the natural seem strange."

"You will remember," says Freud, "that it was a frustration that made the patient ill, and that his *symptoms serve him as substitutive gratifications.*"[24] (Italics mine.) Patients, Freud believed, enjoy their pain and misery, and have a wish to be sick. In fact, he said, it is the "sense of guilt (need for punishment) which binds many neurotics so fast to their neuroses."[25] "With children, it is easy to perceive that they are often 'naughty' on purpose to provoke punishment, and are quiet and contented after the chastisement."[26]

These speculations about troubled consciences in search of self-punishment* have been blended with Freud's death instinct, and an entire literature has sprung up around it. Persons who are accident-prone are supposed to have an unconscious desire to destroy themselves. Automobile drivers in repeated accidents are "turning their aggression inwards" if they hurt only themselves, and "outwards" if they hurt others. Says Dunbar, "For the physician who treats fractures and other bodily injuries several practical issues are of interest. By this time it should be clear that it is

---

* Freud links the "unconscious need for punishment" to being accident-prone in Chapter 4 of his *New Introduction to Psychoanalysis.*

of utmost importance to ask the question as to whether the injury has elements in it other than those of pure accident. In some cases study of circumstances helps but in all cases a careful personality history is important."[27] Dunbar has even enthusiastically said that, "at least 80 per cent of the millions of major accidents [household and factory accidents included] which happen every year" are caused by this unconscious desire for self-destruction.[28]

"In connection with Dunbar's observations concerning the proneness of certain types for accidents [writes W. Horsley Gantt in discussing his highly significant experiments with dogs], it is interesting that Nick showed this [accident-prone] tendency during 1943 as well as previously. In 1937 he frequently got tangled in his chain, binding and hurting himself. In 1943 on the farm, he twice fell into an abandoned privy where he could not extricate himself and where he remained for some hours until he was located by his barking. He would frequently knock into things, get under people's feet, run into machinery, etc. On one occasion at night he followed my car without my knowledge, but as he could not overtake me, I met him on my return homeward. After passing him going in the opposite direction I turned around and went back, but he again had recognized my car and was again running toward me. I put on the brakes, but he continued running into the car which knocked him down and dragged him along, resulting in two scalp wounds. However, he trotted on home at a rapid pace, so that I did not find him until I had also arrived.

"Nick came to an end in January 1944 perhaps

appropriate to his life—he was killed accidentally in a fight with another dog."[29]

Poor Nick! As Gantt said of Nick's other symptoms, "If Nick had been a patient he would undoubtedly have been treated for anxiety attacks and been labelled with the terms merergasia [i.e., neurosis], phobias, gastric neurosis, functional tachycardia, asthma, enuresis [and premature ejaculation]."[30]

A psychoanalyst would probably say that accident-prone Nick felt himself unloved, which made him afraid and neurotic. This in turn gave Nick a feeling of guilt, which in a sense was his anger turning in upon himself, punishing him by masochistic behavior. If the reader thinks I am incoherent I can't blame him—but let me assure him that I have taken this particular reasoning from a recent psychoanalytic explanation of self-defeating behavior in humans. Anybody with morbid curiosity can find dozens of parallels in psychoanalytic literature.

Of course, it is true that certain personalities are more accident-prone than others. The automobile driver who is wrapped up in his daydreams and problems is dangerous at the wheel of his car, and almost everywhere else. To say that a man is preoccupied with his own difficulties and is emotionally withdrawn is the same thing as saying that he cannot get involved with his environment, i.e., that he must be accident-prone—among other things. We need no non-existent death instinct, transformed into an equally nonexistent "unconscious desire for self-destruction," to befog the issue.

As one woman said to me of her psychoanalysis, "I went around worrying all the time, 'What will I do with my unconscious mind, and what will my unconscious mind do with me?' "

Sometimes the analyst refrains from using the Freudian terminology in order not to confuse the patient, but this policy is often self-defeating and makes the patient feel like a purposeless fool. The analytic labels at least help the patient to believe that there is method in his madness, but in that case the patient's constant introspection, which brought him to analysis, is even more intensified. Now the patient watches for signs of his secret purpose to defeat himself, and for the whole demonology of Freudian concepts. Count Keyserling once said, "If all of Germany were at the crossroads and there were two arrows, one saying this way to Heaven, and the other this way to Lectures about Heaven, all the Germans would go to the lectures." Probably lectures on psychoanalysis—many words, but no salvation.

The overwhelming proportion of psychoanalysts, of course, is quite sincere, but sincerity is not what cures patients. "[The] influence of the psychoanalytic therapy," said Freud, "is essentially founded upon transference, i.e., upon suggestion."[31] "And we have to admit that we have only abandoned hypnosis in our methods in order to discover suggestion again in the shape of transference."[32]

And it is by means of the transference that the patient will get a *brand new* neurosis that the analyst will attempt to cure!

It is very easy to establish a transference, said Freud. "The first aim of the treatment consists in attaching him [i.e., the patient] to the treatment and to the person of the physician. To ensure this *one need do nothing but allow him time.* If one devotes serious interest to him, clears away carefully the first resistances that arise and avoids certain mistakes, such an attachment develops in the patient of itself . . ."[33] (Italics mine.) This seems a bit unfair to me, for Freud is saying that the analyst "need do nothing" but allow the patient time. The analyst has only to make a few gestures, control himself slightly, and the helpless patient will develop an attachment for him. The ripe apple will fall into the analyst's lap.

"[The] analyst does nothing to provoke it [i.e., the transference], but on the contrary rather keeps his distance from the patient and maintains a certain reserve in the matter of ordinary personal relationships. . . . This love is in fact *compulsive* [and] . . . this feature always appears in the analytical situation, without any rational explanation."[34]

It was rarely that Freud said something was without "any rational explanation," particularly since he always considered psychoanalytic theories to be a branch of rational explanation. What is more, says Freud, "it is not clear why neurotic subjects under analysis develop the transference so much more intensely than those who are not being analyzed . . ."[35] I think we can supply the reason. The patient in analysis is in an emotionally vulnerable state, and is in great need of help. He is drowning and will hang on for support to any man who looks like a lifesaver. Freud's straight-faced perplexity at why "neurotic subjects under analysis develop the transference so much more intensely than those who are not being analyzed" makes us wonder how he could possibly have overlooked the important role played by the helpless dependency of the confused patient. Freud's oversight becomes even more remarkable when we note that he registered this perplexity at the strength of the transference in helpless neurotics two years after he had said, "Only very few civilized persons are capable of existing without reliance on others or are even capable of coming to an independent opinion. You cannot exaggerate the intensity of man's inner irresolution and craving for authority."[36]

I find it difficult to believe that Freud was not aware of these considerations, but I shall be charitable and say only that Freud probably did not want to emphasize the patient's helplessness in therapy, lest psychoanalysis look like all the other methods of treatment it was supposed to surpass. It is easy to understand the twists and turns of psychoanalytic theory if we keep Freud's early history in mind. In the beginning he worked with hypnosis and suggestion. This was during the age of Queen Victoria, with its strict mores, and Freud became interested in the role of sexuality in the neuroses of his patients. Freud then synthesized the hypnotic theories of his day with his own views on sexuality, and the result was his theory of the neuroses. This historical juxtaposition explains an extraordinary amount of psychoanalytic theory. And the transference, of course, is both sex and suggestion.

Says Freud, "The patient *repeats,* in the form of falling in love with the analyst, psychical experiences which he underwent before; he has *transferred* to the analyst psychical attitudes which lay ready within him."[37] "The fact of the transference appearing, although neither desired nor induced by either physician or patient, in every neurotic who comes under treatment, in its crude sexual, or affectionate, or hostile form, has always seemed to me the most irrefragable proof that the source of the propelling forces of neurosis lies in the sexual life."[38]

Freud once complained to a patient that she refused to form a transference toward him. Said he, to the poetess H. D., when she was not making better progress with her analysis, " 'I am an old man; you do not think it worth your while to love me,' [and] he beat his fists on the table for emphasis."[39] I do not intend the slightest insinuation about Freud. I cite this only to show what a sexual farce is the psychoanalytic transference.

But if the individual who went to be analyzed thought he had troubles before he entered the analyst's office, little does he realize what is going to happen after he gets there. For, said Freud, talking of the transference, "like every love affair, it pushes all other mental activities out of the way; it wipes out interest in the treatment and in improvement, and in short, we can be in no doubt that it has usurped the place of the neurosis, and *our work has had the result of replacing one form of illness by another*."[40] "As soon as the transference [takes hold it] is then not incorrect to say that we no longer have to do with the previous illness, but with a newly created and transformed neurosis which has replaced the earlier one . . . All the patient's symptoms have abandoned their original significance and have adapted themselves to a new meaning. . . . The conquest of this *new artificially acquired neurosis* coincides with the removal of the illness which existed prior to the treatment, that is, with accomplishing the therapeutic task."[41] (Italics mine.) At the risk of belaboring a point, I must repeat what I touched on in the first chapter, and that is the honesty of the analyst who admitted that even if a patient were normal at the beginning of the analysis, the analytic procedure would give him a neurosis.

Freud's complete lack of reality in regard to the transference was shown when he said: "It has come to my knowledge that certain physicians who practise analysis frequently prepare their patients for the advent of a love-transference or even instruct them to 'go ahead and fall in love with the analyst so that the treatment may make progress.' I can hardly imagine a more *nonsensical proceeding*. It robs the phenomenon itself of the element of spontaneity which is so convincing and it lays up *obstacles* ahead which are *extremely difficult to overcome*."[42] (Italics mine.) Even when Freud wrote this, almost every literate psychoanalytic patient knew of the "love-transference." Consequently, Freud's labeling the activity of analysts who prepared their patients for the transference as "nonsensical" applies just as well to his own advice to them. The unreality of this statement is analogous to Freud's advice to analysts that they not indicate any interest in dreams, lest the patient's dreams be affected.

The transference is the method whereby the analyst endeavors to correct the patient's difficulties. No psychoanalyst can possibly question this statement. In Freud's words, ". . . the aim of pleasing the analyst, of winning his applause and his love . . . becomes the true motive-force for the patient's collaboration . . ."[43]

With the harpoon of the transference in the patient, the analyst can give him any interpretation, however preposterous, and the patient will usually go along with it. "Thus the work of analysis involves an art of interpretation, the successful handling of which may require tact and patience but which is *not hard to acquire*."[44] (Italics mine.) Of course the art is not hard to acquire—not when there's a harpoon in the patient.

Freud was once disturbed at the accusation that when analysts give interpretations to a patient—but let me quote Freud—"we treat him upon the famous principle of 'Heads I win, tails you lose.' That is to say, if the patient agrees with us, then the interpretation is right; but if he contradicts us, that is only a sign of his resistance, which again shows that we are right. In this way we are always in the right against the poor helpless wretch whom we are analysing, no matter how he may respond to what we put forward. Now, since it is in fact true that a 'No' from one of our patients is not as a rule enough to make us abandon an interpretation as incorrect, a revelation such as this of the nature of our technique has been most welcome to the opponents of analysis. It is therefore worth while to give a detailed account of how we are accustomed to arrive at an assessment of the 'Yes' or 'No' of our patients during analytic treatment. . . . The practising analyst will naturally learn nothing in the course of this apologia that he does not already know."[45]

And neither will anybody else. Freud's "apologia" repeats the familiar analytic story. The patient "must be got to recollect certain experiences and the emotions called up by them which he has at the moment

forgotten . . . [The] relation of transference . . . is particularly calculated to favor the reproduction of these
emotional connections. . . . What we are in search of
is a picture of the patient's forgotten years . . ."[46] The
psychoanalyst's work "resembles to a great extent an
archaeologist's excavation of some dwelling-place
. . ."[47] And all the rest of it. Freud even says that if
an analyst's interpretation "is wrong, there is no
change in the patient . . ." Only when the analyst "is
right or gives an approximation to the truth" do the
patient's symptoms and general condition become ag-
gravated.[48] On the contrary. I would think that there
would be "an unmistakable aggravation of . . . [a
patient's] symptoms and of his general condition"
when a decent sincere patient, in the grip of the
transference, is convinced that he harbors incestuous
desires for his mother. Such a patient might be completely shattered.

But, said Freud, the analyst must wait for a particular phase of the treatment, before giving interpretations. "When shall we begin our disclosures to the
patient? When is it time to unfold to him the hidden
meaning of his thoughts and associations . . . The
answer to this can only be: Not until a dependable
transference . . . is established in the patient."[49] And
this time Freud was right. Without a firm transference
to the analyst, any patient, listening to the ridiculous
psychoanalytic interpretations of his dreams and free
associations, would laugh so hard that he would roll
right off the couch—and out the waiting room door,
never to be seen again.

"Free association," that is, the unimpeded conversation of the patient, is the analyst's main source of

material. Freud said that this "guarantees to a great extent that . . . nothing will be introduced into . . . [the structure of the neurosis] by the expectations of the analyst."[50] Freud was unduly optimistic.

As we saw in regard to dreams, the analytic situation has a strong effect on what the patient says, and on the interpretation that will be ascribed to it. In the words of Wortis,[51] "It would seem on the surface that the analytic procedure was well suited to promote really free association, and the subject was free from suggestive influences. Actually, however, I think this is not quite the case. The compass of one's interests is very soon cut down to analytic material of immediate interest." Freud admitted this. "We must, however, bear in mind that free association is not really free. The patient remains under the influence of the analytic situation even though he is not directing his mental activities on to a particular subject."[52] This statement does not quite agree with Freud's claim that in free association the patient's "thoughts are not arbitrary but are determined by their reaction to his secret complexes, and may be regarded *to a certain extent* as derived from these complexes."[53] (Italics mine.)

Notice how careful Freud was to say that in free association the patient's thoughts "may be regarded *to a certain extent* as derived from these complexes." No one can argue that *to a certain extent* a patient's personality determines his conversation, but the analytic situation and the analytic processing completely distort whatever the patient may say that happens to be free from the impact of the analytic environment. In the words of Coleman and Commins, even under "the best laboratory procedure, it is virtually impossible to get an unbiased association. Almost anything, even of the most casual nature, a conversation, a dinner, a change in the weather, will change the whole tenor of the subject's associations."[54] One shudders to think what the analytic procedure does to the freedom of "free association."

Free association, concerned as it is with the past, has a tendency to keep the patient's mind away from the present. Instead of removing old grievances, it keeps them fresh and magnified. Simple problems develop the most distressing complications. Fleeting hatreds, that the patient may have felt for his father or mother, become increasingly exaggerated and interfere with his present social relations. Through it all, the patient's immediate and pressing problems receive little attention. To the analyst the present is not very important. For in Freud's words, "the actual conflict of the neurotic becomes comprehensible and *capable of solution* only if it can be traced back to the patient's past history, and by following the path which his libido took when his neurosis started."[55] (Italics mine.)

There we are, dragged back to early sexuality in order to solve *present non*sexual problems. Without a primary emphasis on sex, psychoanalysis is not psychoanalysis at all. Freud never changed the sexual basis of analysis, except in two unimportant regards, but before I discuss them I shall show, with specific statements, Freud's original viewpoint.

The following quotations have been chronologically arranged, and perhaps help to explain why a young man wrote to me that "such aid that I have been able to seek seems to be mainly concerned with my sex life—interesting no doubt, but not helpful."

". . . we have a sexual aetiology in all cases of neurosis," said Freud.[56] "In a little essay on *Anxiety Neurosis* . . . I maintain that neurotic anxiety has its origin in the sexual life . . . The accuracy of this formula has since then been demonstrated with ever-increasing certainty."[57]

"I consider it worth emphasis that, in spite of all changes in them, my views concerning the aetiology of the psychoneuroses have never yet caused me to disavow or abandon two points of view: namely, the importance of sexuality and of infantilism. . . . one learns that the *symptoms represent the patient's sexual activity*, either the whole of it or a part of it . . . Wherever a commonplace emotion must be included among the causative factors of the illness, analysis will regularly show that the pathogenic effect has been exercised by the ever-present sexual element in the traumatic occurrence . . . On the basis of the knowledge acquired by means of psycho-analysis one can only say that the nature of these maladies [the psychoneuroses] lies in disturbances of the sexual processes . . ."[58]

"I can only repeat over and over again—for I never find it otherwise—that sexuality is the key to the problem of the psychoneuroses and of the neuroses in general. No one who disdains the key will ever be able to unlock the door."[59] [Neuroses] "are the specific disorders, so to speak, of the sexual function . . ."[60]

"I have always warned my pupils that our opponents proclaim that we shall come across cases where sexuality plays no part, and we must be strictly on our guard against introducing it into an analysis, lest we miss the chance of finding such a case. None of us has so far had this good fortune."[61]

Soldiers worrying about death. Mothers worrying about children. Men worried about success and failure. Freud sexualized them all.

"With regard to anxious expectation [i.e., "all that is covered by the word 'nervousness' "[62]], clinical experience," said Freud, "has taught us that there is a regular relationship between it and the disposition of the libido in the sexual life."[63] And in the *last book* Freud ever wrote, he said, "The symptoms of neuroses are exclusively, it might be said, either a substitutive satisfaction of some sexual impulse or measures to prevent such a satisfaction, and are as a rule compromises between the two."[64]

Now what were the "modifications" in Freud's theories that persons who want to make psychoanalysis more palatable like to talk about? Briefly, Freud made two subtle distinctions. In his own words, here is the first one: *"It is true that psycho-analysis puts forward lack of sexual satisfaction as the cause of nervous disorders.* But does it not also go much further than this? Is its teaching to be ignored as too complicated when it declares that nervous symptoms arise from a conflict between two forces—on the one hand, the libido (which is for the most part excessive), and on the other, a too severe aversion from sexuality or a repression?"[65] And in somewhat different words, ". . . psycho-analysis has from the very first distinguished the sexual instincts from others which it has provisionally termed 'ego instincts' . . . it has traced back [the neuroses] not to sexuality alone but to the conflict between the sexual impulses and the ego."[66] (Italics mine.)

What lies behind the terminology is not of great import. What Freud is saying is only that *interference* with the patient's sexuality causes neurosis, i.e., "conflict between sexual impulses and the ego." This particular nuance of Freud's fundamental theory, then, is not that sexuality underlies neurosis—but *obstructions* to sexuality underlie neurosis. Well, who ever contended that Freud said otherwise?

It is Freud's second modification of his sexual theories that has some substance. The reader will recall that Freud once postulated Thanatos (the death instinct) as opposed to Eros. This particular modification of Freud's theory says only that psychoanalytic interpretations of the neuroses may involve this death instinct *in addition* to sexuality.

But this drew Freud into another and extremely serious predicament. "In the psycho-analytical theory of the mind," he said, "we take it for granted that the course of mental processes is automatically regulated by 'the pleasure principle,' "[67] i.e., the desire to seek pleasure and to avoid pain—at least, as the psychoanalysts see it. The pleasure principle is the "*sovereign tendency* obeyed by these primary [unconscious] processes . . ."[68] (Italics mine.)

How then can the death (or destructive) instinct be reconciled with the "pleasure principle"? Needless to say, it can't. Says Freud, ". . . satisfaction of what remains in the ego of the death instinct seems not to produce feelings of pleasure [except in the case of masochism . . .]."[69] Then doesn't the invention of the nonexistent death instinct make obsolete *everything* *else* Freud ever wrote? Why, no, says Freud, ". . . most of the impulses of sexual life are not of a purely erotic nature but arise from alloys of the erotic instinct with components of the destructive [i.e., death] instinct."[70] * Here again is the usual Freudian sexuality —sometimes watered down with death instinct, and sometimes just plain undiluted sexuality.

That the death instinct is of *no structural importance whatever* in psychoanalytic theory is demonstrable in another way. As we know, Freud said that repression of the "sex instinct" causes neurosis. Well, if the death instinct with its aggression is as important as Freud's apologists insist, doesn't repression of *that instinct* cause neurosis? The answer is *no*. Says Freud, "Theoretically there is no objection to supposing that any sort of instinctual demand whatever could occasion these same repressions and their consequences; but our observation shows us *invariably,* so far as we can judge, that the excitations that play this pathogenic part arise from the component instincts of sexual life."[71] (Italics mine.)

The inconsistency is extraordinary. If only two instincts, sexuality and the death instinct, are the basis of neurosis in theory, how can *only one instinct—* sexuality—"invariably" be the only basis of neurosis in practice? From the most elementary scientific viewpoint this exposes a deadly contradiction in all of Freud's thinking. Yet all Freud says of this is that "we come upon an interesting discrepancy between theory and experience."[72] It is not pleasant to revise a

* The destructive instinct is synonymous with the "death instinct." It also includes what social workers like to call "hostility" and "aggression."

lifetime of thinking, and it is not easy to revise it without making it even more illogical and contradictory—ergo: "we come upon an interesting discrepancy between theory and experience."

How dare the psychoanalysts and their successors expect to be taken seriously, when they contend that human life is based on two instincts—both of *equal* importance—but that the frustration of *only one of them* (sexuality) is the cause of neurosis! To follow Freud's own theory of repression, if two instincts are of equal importance, both these instincts need full expression. Of sexuality, Freud said in his last book, "neuroses could be avoided . . . if the child's sexual life were allowed free play, as happens among many primitive races."[73] But what of allowing children free expression of their (nonexistent) death instincts? What then? Freud does not discuss this possibility.

Psychoanalysis, as revised, is just as unsound and unscientific as it was in its original form. There has been no change in the belief that *only* sexual repression underlies neurosis. Psychoanalytic theory, as well as practice, remains an inaccurate, and old-fashioned sexual monomania.

But Freud's theory of the death instinct and aggression has brought about one change, and that is in the content of the analytic interview. Now the psychoanalytic grab bag of concepts, long bulging with archaic inaccuracies, has had new booby prizes added to it, which unhappy patients will mistake for the grand prize of understanding and cure.

Freud also tinkered with the therapeutic *aims* of psychoanalysis—but here he could not get very far because he was handicapped by the vulgar facts of history. "Five-and-twenty years of intensive work," said Freud, "have brought about a complete change in the more immediate aims of psycho-analytic technique. At first the endeavours of the analytic physician were confined to divining the unconscious of which his patient was unaware, effecting a synthesis of its various components and communicating it at the right time. Psycho-analysis was above all an art of interpretation."[74] Psychoanalysis, for many years, aimed at "finding out and overcoming the 'resistances,' and we can with justification [said Freud] rely on the complexes coming to light as soon as the resistances have been recognized and removed."[75] "The labour of overcoming the resistances is the essential achievement of the analytic treatment."[76] The analysts would get the unconscious complexes to the surface, and all would be well. It sounded fine, but, as Freud said, ". . . the therapeutic task was not thereby accomplished . . ."[74] We will not talk about what this failure meant to tens of thousands of psychoanalytic patients.

Well, said Freud, "the next aim was to compel the patient to confirm the reconstruction through his own memory. In this endeavour the chief emphasis was on the resistances of the patient; the art now lay in unveiling these as soon as possible, in calling the patient's attention to them, and by human influence—here came in suggestion acting as 'transference'—teaching him to abandon the resistances. It then became increasingly clear, however, that the aim in view, the bringing into consciousness of the unconscious, was not fully attainable by this method either . . ."[74] In the early days of analytic technique it is true that we . . . accounted it specially fortunate if it were possible to

obtain information of the forgotten traumas of childhood from external sources, from parents or nurses,
for instance, or from the seducer himself, as occurred
occasionally; and we hastened to convey the information and proofs of its correctness to the patient, in the
certain expectation of bringing the neurosis and the
treatment to a rapid end by this means. It was a bitter
disappointment when the expected success was not
forthcoming."[77] The revelation of the repressed, the
recapture of the forgotten, the dwelling upon the past
—as therapy they have all failed. Yet to this day the
psychoanalytic approach remains essentially anti-
quarian.

The analyst tries to reconstruct the broken cobwebs
of memory. But, as an example, many individuals with
phobias know where they acquired their fear of blood
or fear of high places. They know it before they go
into treatment, and they know it afterward, yet repressed or not, the old experiences continue to guide
them. In a broad sense, the Freudians believed—and
still believe—that *lack of knowledge about the individual's past is the cause of his present difficulties*, and
that dissolving the "resistances" surrounding those
facts is what cures. As many an analyst (and many a
patient) knows by now, substituting knowledge for
lack of knowledge does the patient no good at all. It
is not freeing the substance of the past that the better-
informed analysts aim at—rather it is removing the
resistance-products of the past. And this—let us call it
"achievement"—they try to accomplish by giving the
patient a *new neurosis* called the transference. Come
gentlemen, really!

The Freudian preoccupation with the past leaves

no serious time for facing the present. Margaret Mead, in a defense of the analytic position, has granted that in an effort to correct "the earlier . . . [non-psychoanalytic] emphasis on 'real conditions,' psychoanalysis has sometimes gone too far in the opposite direction."[78] But as we have seen, it is the very nature of psychoanalytic theory to be completely bound up with the past. As for psychoanalytic therapy, that too must look backward—assuming that analytic principles are the basis of analytic treatment.

But there is a much more important reason why analysts *must* be concerned with the past, and must dwell on it day after day. "At any rate," Freud once said, "one can give a formula for the formation of the ultimate character from the constituent character-traits: the permanent character-traits are either unchanged perpetuations of the original impulses, sublimations of them, or reaction-formations against them."[79]

To put this in clearer language, Freud was saying that an individual's *present* character is based upon:

1. His old antique traits—unchanged. The child who likes to torture dogs becomes an adult who likes to torture dogs. Or,
2. The patient's old antique traits are covered by a socially acceptable veneer—"sublimation." The child who likes to torture dogs becomes an adult who is a surgeon. Or,
3. The patient's old antique traits get transformed by "reaction-formations against them." The child who likes to torture dogs becomes the head of an antivivisection society, or runs a dog haven.

In fact, the very "transference" on which psychoanalysis depends also involves the patient's carrying over his old personality into the present. "[The] patient sees in his analyst the return—the reincarnation—of some important figure out of his childhood or past, and consequently transfers on to him feelings and reactions that undoubtedly applied to this model . . . So long as it [the transference] is positive it serves us admirably."[80]

Psychoanalytic therapy is just as tied to the past as are its patients. The individual has come to the analyst with conscious troubles. The analyst will get after his *unconscious* troubles.

Does the patient feel inferior? This is one of the major complaints of the neurotic individual. To quote Healy, Bronner, and Bowers on Freud's thinking, "The irreconcilability of . . . [Oedipus] wishes with reality and the inadequacy of the childhood stage of development lead to a narcistic scar that constitutes the basis of the inferiority feeling."[81] And to quote Freud, "The sex quest to which the physical development of the child set limits could be brought to no satisfying conclusion"; "hence the plaint in later life, 'I can't do anything, I am never successful.' "[82] In plain language, to the psychoanalysts, inferiority feelings are caused by the child's *inability* to have sexual relations with his mother!

Does the patient have feelings of anxiety like the great majority of neurotics? Does he have feelings of apprehension and tension? Freud used to believe that anxiety was a product of repressed sexuality. This idea permeated 90 per cent of his writings. Freud later changed his mind about this, but the old theoretical implications are still woven through the entire fabric of psychoanalysis. Freud never dropped the idea of repressed sexuality as the basis of neurosis. He merely changed the *procedure* whereby *anxiety* is generated. He moved anxiety out of the id and said that "only the ego can produce and feel anxiety."[83] Besides, said Freud, "It is not the repression that creates the anxiety, but the anxiety . . . creates the repression! But what sort of anxiety can it be? . . . It is the punishment of castration, the loss of his penis."[84] Freud places anxiety under "new" management, and it turns out to be only his old partner Oedipus.

Does the patient feel depressed? "Psychoanalysts have agreed upon [melancholia] as having its roots in oral eroticism,"[85] otherwise called the "cannibalistic stage."

Does a woman have suicidal urges? Freud has it all explained: "That the various means of suicide can represent sexual wish-fulfilments has long been known to all analysts. (To poison oneself = to become pregnant; to drown = to bear a child; to throw oneself from a height = to be delivered of a child.)"[86]

One of Freud's patients spent a great deal of time in squeezing out his blackheads. Why, said Freud, "Analysis shows that he is working out his castration complex upon his skin." Not only that, but, "Pressing out the content of the blackheads is clearly to him a substitute for onanism. The cavity which then appears in consequence of his guilty act is the female genital, *i.e.*, stands for the fulfilment of the threat of castration."[87] Freud does not give a psychoanalytic interpretation of blackhead squeezing in women.

Does a patient suffer from fetishism? Does he hold a lock of hair or a handkerchief from a loved one in great esteem? Or does he perhaps go to peculiar lengths to get objects associated with women? To say that a fetish has come to be *associated* with a female sex object and now is a substitute for it, would make a little sense, but no, says Freud. "When I now disclose that the fetish is a penis-substitute I shall certainly arouse disappointment; so I hasten to add that it is not a substitute for any chance penis, but . . . is a substitute for the woman's (mother's) phallus which the little boy once believed in and does not wish to forego . . ."[88]

The psychoanalysts bear interesting tidings to writers who have lost the urge to write or pianists who don't feel like practicing. "In the case of certain particular inhibitions the trend expressed is rather easily recognized. When *playing the piano, writing,* and even *walking* are made the subject of *neurotic inhibition,* analysis reveals as the basis thereof an excessive erotization of the organ involved in the function in question, the fingers and the feet . . . If writing—which consists in allowing a fluid to flow out from a tube upon a piece of white paper—has acquired the symbolic meaning of coitus, or if walking has become a symbolic substitute for stamping upon the body of Mother Earth, then both writing and walking will be abstained from, because it is as though forbidden sexual behavior were thereby being indulged in."[89] (Italics mine.)

What had Freud to offer for the *phobias,* which, as he said quite correctly, "play so great a part in the symptomatology of the neuroses"?[90] Might claustrophobia be caused by having been locked in a closet? That would be too obvious. Said Freud, "The main point in the problem of phobias seems to me that *phobias do not occur at all when the vita sexualis is normal*."[91] (The italics are Freud's.)

As for children, "The animals which play a part in the animal-phobias of children are generally father-substitutes . . ."[92] Psychoanalysis "often showed that the animal was a substitute for the father, a substitute on to which the fear of the father derived from the Oedipus complex had been displaced."[93] ". . . castration anxiety is given another object and a distorted expression—namely, that of being bitten by a horse (or eaten by a wolf) instead of being castrated by the father."[94] In a few words, "The fear in zoöphobia [fear of animals] is castration anxiety on the part of the ego . . ."[95] Comment is unnecessary, particularly since Freud concluded, "the analysis of phobias which we have undertaken does not seem to be open to correction."[96]

Bed-wetters had a bad time of it with Freud. As children, he said that they regarded suppression of their bed-wetting "as having the meaning of a threat of castration."[97] And when they grew up, and were psychoanalyzed, Freud detected in them, as a definite consequence of their bed-wetting, an "intense 'burning' ambition."[98] Let me again assure the reader that Freud was quite serious about all this. Some of his recent disciples have said that bed-wetting, when it is a neurotic symptom, "is the manifestation of a bisexual tendency. Both boys and girls suffer from night terror, the content of which is the fear of being attacked by an adult of the opposite sex. The fear mobilizes the sado-masochistic excitation which is discharged by urination."[99]

The reader can guess what the results of psycho-analytic treatment must be, based as it is on the theories and practices we have been considering. As an example, A. A. Brill,[100] Freud's leading American disciple and translator, said of treating stuttering by psychoanalysis: " '[My] enthusiasm declined with the length of my experience.' He says that in eleven years he handled 600 cases, analysed 69, and claims to have cured only 4."

The patient has come to analysis with problems, and he talks—and talks and talks some more. And the analyst? He listens—and listens and listens again. Landis,[101] for instance, reported that in 221 hours of analysis, his analyst spent *2 per cent of the time* in discussing the material that he brought forth. This averages down to a little over *one minute of discussion by the analyst in every analytic hour*.

The analysts contend that the intellectual content of an analysis is not as important as the "emotional interchanges" between analyst and patient. We can grant this, and still say that it is highly questionable whether much can be accomplished in the infinitesimal time devoted to emotional give and take. And the analysts might as well face it, but many of them are rather stuffy and not particularly able to stimulate their patients. Yet they do not have to, for, as we saw earlier, all that the analyst has to do is to sit tight until the patient has formed a transference. Freud has even said that, in treating certain neurotic compulsions, "I think there is little doubt that here the correct technique can only be to wait until the treatment itself has become a compulsion, and then with this counter-compulsion forcibly to suppress the compulsion of the disease."[102] Here is the transference in its rawest form. Put your hooks into the patient and then you can do anything.

While undergoing analysis, the patient is expected to remain in the *status quo*. He is not to change jobs or wives or friends or anything else during treatment. Analysts have been known to use the fact that a patient made a change in his living pattern as an excuse for the failure of treatment. This seems to me a specious objection, for even if the patient made another neurotic change while undergoing treatment, I think it is ridiculous to try to keep therapy and life separate. As Wertham said, analysts "have their patients lead a double existence—half lying on a couch and half standing up to life—and are unable to unite the two existences constructively."[103] Patients lead a single life, and analytic therapy, *without any fundamental emphasis on problems now*, must be labeled as being out of touch with reality.

The analytic patient always runs into serious difficulties at home, beyond those that may have contributed to his seeking treatment. But with all this, he can at least lean on the analyst. His wife, however, has no one to fall back upon. To her the analyst assumes the role of an intruder who is trying to rob her of her husband. She gets the feeling that here is a variation of the eternal triangle—husband, wife, and psychoanalyst. She knows that everything she says and does is being hashed over with the analyst, and she may feel that the analysis seems more important to her husband than she does.

Now there is no question that a wife whose husband

is being analyzed usually acts most unfairly to the analyst. Out loud, she may blame him for her husband's distress, and in her heart she may wonder to what extent she herself is responsible for her husband's condition, and whether, when the analysis is over, her marriage will remain. She may accuse her husband of using his analysis as a form of self-indulgence, and sometimes she may even be foolish enough to believe that her husband would get better if he would "just quit worrying so much, and knuckle down and be practical." In my opinion, all these objections are unfair. Psychological difficulties cannot be solved by homilies and friendly bromides. But the fact remains that the tortured relatives of those in analysis have one particularly valid point, and that is that they are the victims of the unrealism that permeates psychoanalytic therapy. These relatives are the victims of the preoccupation with the past that the analysts advocate—which fallacious preoccupation the analysts have misnamed "deep therapy."

At any rate, the analysis continues. Weeks turn into months, and more often into years. Milner reports a case in which after *five* years of psychoanalysis both patient and analyst agreed that the treatment had failed.[104] However, it was also reported that improvement in this patient took place after the analysis had been terminated, and presumably as a result of the patient's earlier psychoanalysis. This delayed improvement may sometimes occur, but in an analysis it is always easy for the analyst to take credit for improvements that were really caused by changes in the patient's altered way of life. Psychoanalysis is so long-drawn-out that patients have a chance to undergo many favorable changes in their lives and circumstances—for which improvements the analyst may take the credit quite sincerely, but most inaccurately.

All of which raises an important question. Precisely *when* is an analysis over? Freud has said clearly enough, "An analysis is ended when analyst and patient cease to meet for the analytic session."[105] Surely no one can argue with this definition. Of course, what is more important about the termination of an analysis is how much happier is the patient? Says Freud in this regard, "First, the patient must no longer be suffering from his former symptoms and must have overcome his various anxieties and inhibitions and, secondly, *the analyst must have formed the opinion* [italics mine] that so much repressed material has been brought into consciousness, so much that was inexplicable elucidated, and so much inner resistance overcome that no repetition of the patient's specific pathological processes is to be feared."[106]

I don't think there is any question that in many analyses a good deal of the patient's repressed memories are brought into consciousness, many explanations, however psychoanalytic, are made of the patient's behavior, much of the patient's "inner resistance" (what terms!) is overcome, and factual memories and the emotions attached to them are brought to the surface. I say that I do not doubt that this happens in many analyses. All I question is whether the patient, who has spent a great deal of money, and two or more years of his life in treatment, and has recalled the time he smoked his first cigarette behind the ash bin, and how he learned about sex from Matilda next door; or—in the case of a woman—that she hates men deep down in her heart because they remind her of her father, and therefore she tries to punish them for her father's lack of affection, and now hates her son for it—to repeat, all I question is whether the patient who has learned all this feels especially better. As people have told me of their analyses all too often, "When the story of my life was finished, and my tale of woe done, there was simply nothing new to say except to voice my resentment at the futility of the whole procedure and quit."

Terminating analysis is not easy, because the transference has to be dissolved. As Freud said, ". . . the greatest adroitness in handling the 'transference' is required . . . You will see that this point represents the culminating demands upon analytic technique. It is here that one may make the gravest mistakes or achieve the greatest success. It would be senseless to attempt to evade difficulties by suppressing or ignoring the transference; whatever else may have been done up to this point could not deservedly be called an analysis. To send the patient away, so soon as the awkwardness of his transference-neurosis came into play, would be absurd, and cowardly as well; it would be as though *one were to summon up spirits, and then run away when they appeared. Sometimes, indeed, there is nothing else to be done; there are cases in which the transference, once unleashed, cannot be mastered, and the analysis must then be broken off.*"[107] (Italics mine.) Here indeed is witchcraft masquerading as science—a sexually based dependence subtly "unleashed," and then, when it "cannot be mastered, and the analysis must then be broken off," the patient is consigned to outer darkness.

Another analyst has said that psychoanalysis may be terminated even though a "residue of infantile cravings will continue to exist."[108] It can easily be more than a residue, for, as we have seen, the entire analytic procedure fosters the most complete and dangerous sort of dependence. This explains to us why many patients find it difficult to break off their analyses, and become as habituated to treatment as if it were a narcotic.

Many patients never complete analysis. They grow tired of it. But let us assume that a patient eventually completes his treatment. What then?

We have all read of certain theatrical personalities who have been psychoanalyzed for many years and who constantly talk about it to interviewers. They talk most amusingly, yet it seems that although the psychoanalysis was a success, the patient remains unhappy. Life still has no savor, they are still beset by worry and insomnia.

Sometimes the analytically treated patient strikes his friends like the man in the cartoon who is standing on his head, quite naked, and blowing a trumpet in the midst of a great crowd. Says the caption, "Of course I'm cured." As a man I treated put it, "I have seen about twenty people at different times who have been thoroughly psychoanalyzed—at least they said so —and that convinced me against analysis more than any theoretical objections."

Many individuals have a fabulous glibness after being psychoanalyzed. They are filled with words— about self-punishment, anxiety, hostility, and rationalization. *They* never rationalize. They *know*, for they now have *insight*.

In my opinion, insight is the tombstone of psychoanalysis, for insight is not necessarily accompanied by important symptom improvement. Often, individuals with insight might as well be saying, "My dentist is marvelous. My teeth still ache, but I know all about my roots and my root canals. I can even read my own X-rays . . . Really, you should try my dentist." Such persons remain as entranced with psychoanalysis as the analysts themselves, and continue to look down their noses at other approaches that would do them more good. Some of them are shunned by their friends, for they seem unable to talk about anything except analysis, and are constantly analyzing everybody's motives.

Some of these persons might be called "the smugly psychoanalyzed." They consider themselves members of a select group of sophisticates and act as if those who have not undergone analysis, or who mock its pretensions, have intelligence quotients at least 40 points below theirs. Of course, they're the ones who say that only the analyzed dare talk about analysis. "Yes," they say learnedly. "A little knowledge is a dangerous thing. What you are saying is a sign that you are unqualified to judge, but someday you will change your mind." And the more casual they are, the greater is their snobbery.

Many persons go to analysts and learn a set of names for their ailments, and consider it therapy. One of the terms that most analytic patients pick up is "ambivalent." For example, "I feel ambivalent about going to the theater. I want to go, and then again, I don't want to go." As one such person said to me, "At least I picked up some patter. You don't even get a vocabulary for your money with the silent analysts."

In an analysis the individual gets no sudden ray of blinding revelation. It is more of a day-to-day grind, and when it is over, he may say, "I find myself full of knowledge about myself and my goals and my life, but without any power to do anything with this knowledge." Or, as someone else said, "I see now that my analysis helped very little, except to better my understanding of my reactions." When the individual entered analysis he suffered from certain feelings and didn't know why. Now he thinks he knows why.

The analyst who contends that he has shown his patients how to understand their problems has usually done something quite different. I think one of the most pernicious features of psychoanalysis is that it makes many individuals what I would call *perceptively neurotic*. The patient remains as introspective as ever, but he now has verbal formulae for every occasion. He has an increased (psychoanalytic) awareness of his mental processes, but he is still engaged in the same contemplation of the mosaic of himself that brought him to analysis. The new terms that he has learned for his *new awarenesses* should not blind us to the fact that in essence he is still preoccupied with himself.

Yet many of those who talk of the wonders of analysis must, in the still, silent hours of the morning, have their doubts. It is not easy for them to admit to themselves that at the cost of considerable time, money, and effort, they have, as the phrase goes, been had. They cling tenaciously to a belief in their analysis and close their eyes to their own later judgment and to that of their friends. The result is that they act like Judas-goats in the stockyards, leading their friends to the slaughter.

For psychoanalysis fails again and again, and it is not always the patient's fault. I will grant that there are certain problems in which any form of present treatment can do very little, and that the analyst should not be blamed for his failure with them. Simple-appearing neuroses may turn out to be extremely deep and inaccessible psychiatric conditions, and the environment of the patient may weave such a web that it is impossible to liberate him. But setting all this aside, there still remain a tremendous number of persons who have been hurt by analysis. It is not possible to accept Freud's statement that "serious and lasting aggravation of a neurotic illness is not to be feared from incompetent employment of analysis. The disagreeable reactions soon die down."[109] I say that this statement is false, for every analyst, psychiatrist, and psychologist has met people who wear the saber scars of "incompetent analysis." And many indeed are the people who, after presumably *competent* analysis, seem more distressed than they were before. Wertham has given a perfect name to their affliction. He calls it "post-analytic invalidism."

As an example, I could cite the case of the fine young actor who told everybody how psychoanalysis had cured him, but who died after receiving sedation for an anxious state. After his death it was learned that he had been under intensive treatment for two years after announcing his psychoanalytic cure. Or I could cite the case of the gifted young singer who said in print of her psychoanalytic experience, "I have never regretted anything more."

Let me repeat that I am not saying that even excellent psychotherapy, in its present state, can cure everybody. I am only trying to point out that the therapeutic claims of psychoanalysis have been incredibly exaggerated and are most unjustified. Of course psychoanalysts have their cures—but is it due to the incredible theory called psychoanalysis, or is it because a decent and sympathetic human being puts psychoanalysis on the shelf and extends a hand to his patient? As Myerson said, "The neuroses are 'cured' by osteopathy, chiropractic, nux vomica and bromides, benzedrine sulfate, change of scene, a blow on the head, and psychoanalysis, which probably means that none of these has yet established its real worth in the matter, and surely that psychoanalysis is no specific."[110]

Statistics on the results of psychoanalytic therapy are not very impressive. Recently, Wertham, after many years of experience, said that 60 per cent of psychoanalyses are "more harmful than helpful," and that four out of five analyses "are not indicated."[111]

In England, E. B. Strauss' figures, published in the *British Journal of Medical Psychology,* are even more disillusioning. He concluded that ". . . in the best hands, the psychoanalytic *method* will continue to 'cure' its twenty-two to twenty-five percent of selected cases, devoting four to five sessions per week for months and even years on end to the individual patient."[112]

The most comprehensive set of statistics on the results of psychoanalytic therapy are those of

Knight.[113] He presents a study of psychoanalytic results with 952 patients. The combined figures come from the Berlin Psychoanalytic Institute, from a published study of Hyman and Kessel,[114] from the London Psychoanalytic Clinic, from the Chicago Psychoanalytic Institute, and from the Menninger Clinic. In discussing Knight's summary I shall omit results with psychotics, psychopaths, epileptics, and "organ neuroses and organic conditions."* In cases of this nature, failures should not be held against analysis. The only cases which need concern us are 736 cases labeled as psychoneurotics, "sexual disorders," character disorders, etc. Just what were the results of analytic treatment, as reported, in almost all cases, *by the analysts themselves?*

Total number of cases   736
Number of cases in which
   treatment was broken off
   before six months . . . .   205, i.e., 27.8%

Here is our first observation. Twenty-seven and eight-tenths per cent of the psychoanalytic patients quit before six months were over. Although they may well have included many curiosity-seekers, we can be sure that they also included some people who became fed up with analysis. Knight says of this 27.8 per cent of patients, "the excluded cases, *i.e.*, those treated less than six months, represent an important group of 'failures.' " Putting it approximately, *3 out of 10 analytic patients are failures within six months.*

Number of cases treated
   six months or longer . . . . .   531, i.e., 72.1%

* These include most of the "more severe cases" referred to by Appel in his discussion of this study.[115]

Which leads us to another observation. The cases who were treated six months or longer had become a more carefully selected group. Many of them may have felt some improvement, and consequently were remaining under analytic treatment. Consequently, with this group, the cards are definitely stacked in favor of analysis. Nevertheless, this group also had its failures. The failures were of two kinds—results that were hardly worth the effort, described by Knight as "those patients who were slightly or only moderately better at the end of the treatment, but in whom the improvement was of lesser degree [than those called "much improved"] and [whose improvement] might be attributable to other factors than the treatment."

Number of cases in which
   improvement was apparent
   but *not significant*   158

Add to this the

Number of cases labeled
   "no change or worse"   54

Knight combines these two
   categories as failures,
   but we may add, in addition
   to these, the patients who
   did *not* continue after 6
   months of analysis and who,
   Knight said, "represent an important group of 'failures.' "   205

            Total   417

This means, then, that 417 out of 736 patients were not helped at all by analysis, i.e., *psychoanalysis was a failure with 56.7 per cent of patients.*

Knight also reported that 157 patients were "apparently cured." I am in full agreement with his criteria for cure, and I do not doubt these results at all. Add to these patients 162 patients who were "much improved," i.e., "those cases in which improvement was considerable and was attributable to the analysis, but in which the analyst felt that a complete cure was lacking in some respects," as I said, add

Apparent cures   157
Much improved   162
                                    ———
             Total   319

This means, then, that 319 out of 736 patients were helped by analysis, i.e., *psychoanalysis was definitely helpful to 43.3 per cent of patients.*

Putting it all concisely, in this extensive study of the results of the psychoanalytic treatment of 736 people, *psychoanalysis was a failure with 56.7 per cent of the patients, and a definite success with 43.3 per cent of the patients. Psychoanalysis failed somewhat more often than it succeeded.*

As Appel[116] said of this same study, "The statistical results of psychoanalytic treatment . . . of the psychoneuroses differ little from those of other methods of therapy."

And if that is the case, why should we have any particular respect for psychoanalysis? Analysts are would-be scientists, practicing an embryo profession, with an unimpressive percentage of cures. And not only is psychoanalysis time-consuming and expensive, but it is a frightening and complicated way of doing what other methods of treatment do at least as well.

We can say of psychoanalysis what the farmer once said. "A big cloud, but very little rain."

I think it is of tremendous importance that we develop sounder forms of therapy. Now more people than ever are mentally ill, and the backwash of war has added to the problem. Long-drawn-out and anemic psychoanalysis could never begin to catch up with the backlog of cases in a thousand years. What is to be done?

The picture is not favorable, but there are a few bright spots. First, there has been a revolt within psychoanalysis itself. A group of analysts in Chicago, under Alexander and French, have reached the conclusion that the important thing for the mentally disturbed individual is to change his conduct with people. In order to overcome the effects of his unfortunate early experiences, he needs new and healthy emotional experiences in the present. This breath of fresh air in the stifling psychoanalytic atmosphere indicates an awareness that the way to get rid of old habits is to get new habits. Though they practice short-term therapy, the so-called Chicago school has not sufficiently dumped the Freudian terminology and concepts. It is to be hoped that in time they will discard their Freudian excess baggage and advance even further. The same is true of the work of Dollard and Miller at Yale. They too remain strait-jacketed by Freudian theory. Other analysts, like Fromm and Horney, have also discarded a great deal of the Freudian extravagances and have an approach to therapy that is more in keeping with reality than that of standard analysis.*

* This was particularly true of the late Harry Stack Sullivan.

But they all are essentially based on permutations and combinations of Freud. They all lower buckets into the well-nigh bottomless pit of Freudian ambiguity and try to dredge up some sense. And whatever they have from healthier scientific sources they well-meaningly soil with muddy Freudian hands. Estes has spoken aptly of the "solemn overstriving to convince the reader that the revised formulations and procedures *are* psychoanalytic."[117]

In my opinion, the way out of the impasse of modern psychotherapy has nothing to do with psychoanalysis. For while the Freudian vapors of death instinct and sexual obscurantism hung in a heavy atomic cloud over most of psychiatry, in the laboratories of most of our colleges and universities a new and healthy psychology was being developed. At no time was it deceived by the transient Freudian popularity. At all times it realized one thing, and that is that, broadly speaking, human emotional problems are the result of personal mis-education. It always believed that only by learning new emotional habits could the neurotic individual learn to be happy. More to the point, at all times the leaders of this trend were insistent upon checking the truth of their findings against large groups of people, and not just talking off the cuff in the Freudian metaphysical way.

It seems to me, the healthiest trend of all in the college and university work has been the recognition that, for practical therapeutic purposes, the human being is largely a habit machine. Here the thinking of Pavlov presents the most hopeful opportunities for the rapid and deep modification of human personality. Elsewhere I have written in great detail in regard to this approach.[118] Here I will say that in essence Pavlov's *conditioned reflex therapy* declares that fundamentally *everybody has the same problem and the same cure*. I can illustrate this principle by some situations encountered in therapy:

Dr. A. is a dentist, and is afraid of blood.

Mr. B. has claustrophobia, and is afraid of elevators.

Miss C. is an actress, and finds it difficult to face an audience.

Mrs. D. is a writer who cannot concentrate on her work.

Mr. E. says that life isn't worth living.

Some of these people were brought up in the country, and some in the city. Some had kind fathers, some had stern ones. Some were indulged by their mothers, and some were frequently punished. Some were jealous of an older brother, and some were not. Some were only children, some were the youngest, and some were the oldest. In short, these people had entirely different histories and, presumably, entirely different problems.

After taking a phenobarbital pill, or a stiff drink, Dr. A., the dentist, does not mind blood at all.

Mr. B. rides comfortably in his office elevator.

Miss C. finds it easy to appear before an audience.

Mrs. D. sits down at the typewriter and works for two hours.

Mr. E. decides that the world is a fairly interesting place after all.

To be sure, the problems return when the phenobarbital or alcohol wears off, but five different persons, with five different problems, stemming from five different pasts, have been temporarily "cured" by one and the same thing. What other conclusion seems possible, save that all five suffer from essentially the *same* disturbance.

There can be no question that therapy is quick and simple once the therapist realizes that the underlying problem of mental illness is always exactly the same. Then the individual is spared the futile pain of wandering blindly through the swamps of early experiences. But I have not written this book to explain conditioned reflex therapy. I will just say, at this point, that at all times the emphasis is on the individual's present—the things he's doing now. Cure comes through learning healthy PERSONAL RELATIONSHIPS NOW, and not by stewing over past emotional frustrations.

In the words of Snygg and Combs, "If present perceptions govern behavior, psychotherapy must concern itself with present perceptions rather than genetic understandings. It is the understanding and implementation of this point which probably represents the most important single difference between client-centered therapy and traditional psychoanalysis."[119] Snygg and Combs relate a little anecdote about the six-year-old daughter of one of them which is worth repeating.

> " 'Why did you do that, Frances?' she was asked.
>   'Oh, my brain told me to do it.'
>   'Well, why did your brain tell you to do it?'
>   'Oh (with a giggle), I guess its brain told it to do it.' "

"Such explanatory constructs are fairly common . . . but they have never been very fruitful . . . [The psychoanalytic] ego is a much more sophisticated construct than the 'brain's brain' but they are both second order constructs set up to explain the first order constructs which are set up to explain the observed behavior. In effect they are attempts to explain a mystery by a greater mystery."

Psychotherapy is in a state of transition, and psychoanalysis, in all of its manifold disguises, brings nothing but confusion in our efforts to arrive at a real science of human behavior.

William James made some remarks over a half century ago about Fechner, the great nineteenth-century psychologist. It is incredible to realize how true these comments are when applied to Freud. If we substitute "Freud" for "Fechner" (whom Freud admired), and apply James' remarks to the matter at hand, they would read like this:[120]

"Freud's books were the starting point of a new department of literature, which it would be perhaps impossible to match for the qualities of thoroughness and subtlety, but of which, in the humble opinion of the present writer, the proper psychological outcome is just *nothing*. The Freudian Unconscious and the conception of it as an ultimate 'psychological discovery' will remain an 'idol of the den' if ever there was one. Freud himself indeed was a Teutonic *Gelehrter* of the ideal type, at once simple and shrewd, a mystic and an experimentalist, homely and daring, and loyal to facts that fitted his theories.

"But it would be terrible if this man could saddle psychology forever with his patient whimsies, and, in a world so full of more nutritious objects of attention, compel all future students to plough through the difficulties, not only of his own works, but of the still drier ones written in his support. The only amusing part of it is that Freud's supporters should always feel bound, after smiting his theories hip and thigh and leaving not a stick of them standing, to wind up by saying that nevertheless to him belongs the *imperishable glory* of first formulating them and thereby turning psychology into a *science*(!)."

REFERENCES

Two references in this bibliography call for particular mention. Healy, Bronner, and Bowers' *Structure and Meaning of Psychoanalysis* has been an invaluable compendium of Freudiana. The five-volume *Collected Papers of Sigmund Freud*, published by the Hogarth Press, Ltd., London, is an almost complete collection of Freud's less accessible writings which have appeared in otherwise scattered sources.

In quoting from Freud I have tried to confine my references to the most currently available editions, rather than to relatively inaccessible earlier printings.

PREFACE

1. I have taken this sentence almost verbatim from p. 108 of: EISSLER, K. R. "The Chicago Institute of Psychoanalysis and the Sixth Period of the Development of Psychoanalytic Technique," *Journal of General Psychology*, 1950, 42:103-157.

CHAPTER 1

The Twilight of Psychoanalysis

1. FREUD, S. *Collected Papers.* (The Hogarth Press, London, 1950), V, 382.

2. LANDIS, C. "Psychoanalytic Phenomena," *Journal of Abnormal and Social Psychology*, 1940, 35:17-28.

3. BORING, E. G. "Was This Analysis a Success?" *Journal of Abnormal and Social Psychology*, 1940, 35:4-10.

4. JONES, E. *Papers on Psychoanalysis*. Quoted in: HINSIE, L. E., and SHATZKY, J. *Psychiatric Dictionary* (with "Encyclopedic Treatment of Modern Terms"). (Oxford University Press, New York, 1940), p. 486.

5. Quoted in: LUDWIG, E. *Dr. Freud*. (Hellman Williams and Company, New York, 1947), p. 72.

6. FREUD, S. *Collected Papers*, III, 429-430.

7. HINSIE, L. E., and SHATZKY, J. *Op. cit.*, p. 83.

8. SEARS, R. R. *Survey of Objective Studies of Psychoanalytic Concepts*. Social Science Research Council, Bulletin 51, New York, 1943.

9. ———. *Ibid.*, p. 133.

10. ———. *Ibid.*, p. 134.

11. ———. *Ibid.*, p. x.

12. JASTROW, J. *Freud, His Dream and Sex Theories*. (World Publishing Company, Cleveland, 1932), p. 293.

13. MYERSON, A. "The Attitude of Neurologists, Psychiatrists and Psychologists towards Psychoanalysis," *American Journal of Psychiatry*, 1939, 96:623-641.

14. FREUD, S. *An Outline of Psychoanalysis*. (W. W. Norton and Company, New York, 1949), p. 9.

15. ROHEIM, G. (Editor). *Psychoanalysis and the Social Sciences*. (International Universities Press, New York, 1948), p. 32.

16. JASTROW, J. *Op. cit.*, pp. 265-66.

17. ROHEIM, G. *Op. cit.*

18. FREUD, S. "The History of the Psychoanalytic Movement." In *The Basic Writings of Sigmund Freud*. Translated and edited by A. A. Brill. (Modern Library, Random House, New York, 1938), p. 951.

19. Quoted in: MANGAN, S. "The French Turn to Psy-

choanalysis: Freud Breaches Reason's Citadel," *Commentary*, February, 1950:182-188.

20. FREUD, S. "The History of the Psychoanalytic Movement," *op. cit.*, p. 952.

21. HEALY, W., BRONNER, A. F., and BOWERS, A. M. *The Structure and Meaning of Psychoanalysis.* (Alfred A. Knopf, New York, 1930), p. 346.

22. FREUD, S. *New Introductory Lectures on Psycho-Analysis.* (W. W. Norton and Company, New York, 1933), p. 230.

23. GRAVES, R. "A Motley Hero," *The Sewanee Review*, Autumn, 1949, LVII, No. 4:698-702.

24. ESTES, S. G. *Journal of Abnormal and Social Psychology*, 1947, 42:142.

CHAPTER 2

The Dictatorship of the Unconscious

1. FREUD, S. *Beyond the Pleasure Principle.* (The Hogarth Press, London, 1948), p. 76. Joseph Jastrow's translation of this passage is given on p. 293 of his *Freud, His Sex and Dream Theories* (World Publishing Company, Cleveland, 1932), and I have used his rendering because it is somewhat more accurate and felicitous.

2. HEALY, W., BRONNER, A. F., and BOWERS, A. M. *The Structure and Meaning of Psychoanalysis.* (Alfred A. Knopf, New York, 1930), p. 152.

3. FREUD, S. *New Introductory Lectures on Psycho-Analysis.* (W. W. Norton and Company, New York, 1933), p. 170.

4. ———. *Ibid.*, pp. 170-171.

5. ———. *Ibid.*, p. 175.

6. ———. *Ibid.*, p. 176.

7. FREUD, S. *An Outline of Psychoanalysis.* (W. W. Norton and Company, New York, 1949), p. 99.

8. ———. *Ibid.,* p. 97.

9. ———. *New Introductory Lectures on Psycho-Analysis,* p. 165.

10. ———. *Ibid.,* p. 164.

11. ———. *An Autobiographical Study.* (The Hogarth Press and The Institute of Psycho-Analysis, London, 1946), pp. 60-61.

12. HEALY, W., BRONNER, A. F., and BOWERS, A. M. *Op. cit.,* p. 129: "Ernest Jones says of the Oedipus complex that it is 'the most characteristic and important finding in all psychoanalysis . . .' "

13. FREUD, S. *Collected Papers.* (The Hogarth Press, London, 1950), I, 350-351.

14. ———. *New Introductory Lectures on Psycho-Analysis,* pp. 180-181.

15. ———. *Ibid.,* p. 175.

16. ———. *The Problem of Anxiety.* (W. W. Norton and Company, New York, 1936), p. 67.

17. ———. *New Introductory Lectures on Psycho-Analysis,* pp. 182-183.

18. ———. *Ibid.,* p. 182.

19. ———. *Ibid.,* p. 183.

20. ———. *Ibid.,* p. 158.

21. ———. *An Outline of Psychoanalysis,* pp. 90-91.

22. ———. *Collected Papers,* V, 120.

23. ———. *Ibid.,* III, 583.

24. MENNINGER, W. C. "An Analysis of Psychoanalysis," *The New York Times Sunday Magazine,* May 18, 1947, pp. 12, 48.

25. JUNG, C. G. *Contributions to Analytic Psychology.* (Harcourt Brace and Company, New York, 1928), p. 340.

26. FREUD, S. *The Question of Lay Analysis.* (W. W. Norton and Company, New York, 1950), p. 53.

27. FREUD, S. "Three Contributions to the Theory of Sex." In *The Basic Writings of Sigmund Freud*. Translated and edited by A. A. Brill. (The Modern Library, Random House, New York, 1938), p. 625.

28. ———. *The Question of Lay Analysis*, p. 54.

29. KANNER, L. *In Defense of Mothers*. (Charles C. Thomas, Springfield, Illinois, 1941), pp. 132-133.

30. ———. *Ibid*. Kanner's two quotations are from Freud's "Three Contributions to the Theory of Sex," *op. cit.*, p. 597.

31. FREUD, S. *The Problem of Anxiety*, p. 34.

32. ———. *Collected Papers*, V, 266.

33. ———. *New Introductory Lectures on Psycho-Analysis*, p. 99.

34. ———. *An Outline of Psychoanalysis*, p. 37.

35. ———. *Collected Papers*, V, 382.

36. MAIER, N. R. F. *Frustration, the Study of Behavior Without a Goal*. (McGraw-Hill Book Company, New York, 1949), p. 242.

37. HEALY, W., BRONNER, A. F., and BOWERS, A. M. *Op. cit.*, p. 35.

38. FREUD, S. *An Outline of Psychoanalysis*, p. 19.

39. ———. *Ibid.*, p. 108.

40. ———. *Ibid.*, p. 62.

41. Quoted in: LUDWIG, E. *Dr. Freud*. (Hellman Williams and Company, New York, 1947), p. 79.

42. FREUD, S. *The Problem of Anxiety*, p. 24.

43. ———. *New Introductory Lectures on Psycho-Analysis*, p. 108.

44. ———. *Ibid.*, p. 104.

45. ———. *Ibid.*, p. 84.

46. ———. *The Question of Lay Analysis*, p. 80.

47. ———. *An Outline of Psychoanalysis*, p. 19.

48. ———. *An Autobiographical Study*, p. 58.

49. SCHAFER, R. *Journal of Abnormal and Social Psychology*, 1950, 45, No. 1:187.

50. SEARS, R. R. *Survey of Objective Studies of Psychoanalytic Concepts.* Social Science Research Council, Bulletin 51, New York, 1943, p. 143.

51. FREUD, S. *An Outline of Psychoanalysis,* p. 92.

52. MULLAHY, P. *Oedipus Myth and Complex.* (Hermitage Press, New York, 1948) , p. 271.

53. ———. *Ibid.*

54. WESTERMARCK, E. *Three Essays on Sex and Marriage.* (Macmillan and Company, London, 1934) .

55. MULLAHY, P. *Op. cit.,* pp. 323-324.

56. ———. *Ibid.,* p. 270.

57. BATESON, G. "Cultural Determinants of Personality." In *Personality and the Behavior Disorders.* Edited by J. McV. Hunt. (The Ronald Press Company, New York, 1944) , II, 727.

58. FREUD, S. *An Outline of Psychoanalysis,* pp. 112-113.

59. ———. *Beyond the Pleasure Principle,* p. 47.

60. ———. *Ibid.,* editorial preface.

61. ———. *Ibid.,* pp. 63-64.

62. ———. *Ibid.,* p. 48.

63. ———. *Ibid.*

64. MORGAN, C. T. *Physiological Psychology.* (McGraw-Hill Book Company, New York, 1943) , p. 396.

65. BERNARD, L. L. "Instinct." *Encyclopedia of the Social Sciences.* (Macmillan Company, New York, 1937), VIII, 81-83.

66. FREUD, S. *Beyond the Pleasure Principle,* p. 45.

67. MORGAN, C. T. *Op. cit.,* pp. 396-411.

68. BERNARD, L. L. "Instinct," *op. cit.*

69. FREUD, S. *Beyond the Pleasure Principle,* pp. 44-45.

70. Quoted by PUNER, H. W. *Freud, His Life and His Mind.* (Grosset and Dunlap, New York, 1947), pp. 210-211.

71. FREUD, S. *Civilization and Its Discontents.* (The Hogarth Press, London, 1950) , p. 94.

72. FREUD, S. *New Introductory Lectures on Psycho-Analysis,* pp. 144-145.
73. ———. *Collected Papers,* II, 95.
74. This first appeared in *Die Fackel* (Vienna) in June, 1913.

CHAPTER 3

The Bitter Fruit

1. FREUD, S. *Collected Papers.* (The Hogarth Press, London, 1950), V, 329.
2. ———. *Collected Papers,* II, 349.
3. KUBIE, L. S. *Practical and Theoretical Aspects of Psychoanalysis.* (International Universities Press, New York, 1950), pp. 37, 39.
4. FREUD, S. *Collected Papers,* II, 354.
5. FROMM-REICHMANN, F. *Principles of Intensive Psychotherapy.* (The University of Chicago Press, 1950), p. 10.
6. FREUD, S. *Collected Papers,* II, 331.
7. ———. *Ibid.,* p. 327.
8. LANDIS, C. "Psychoanalytic Phenomena," *Journal of Abnormal and Social Psychology,* 1940, 35:26.
9. KUBIE, L. S. *Op. cit.,* p. 227.
10. SALTER, A. *Conditioned Reflex Therapy.* (Farrar, Straus and Young, New York, 1949), p. 56.
11. FREUD, S. *A General Introduction to Psycho-Analysis.* (Perma Giants, New York, 1949), p. 376.
12. Quoted by HEALY, W., BRONNER, A. F., and BOWERS, A. M. *The Structure and Meaning of Psychoanalysis.* (Alfred A. Knopf, New York, 1930), p. 434.
13. MYERSON, A. *Speaking of Man.* (Alfred A. Knopf, New York, 1950), p. 67.

14. FREUD, S. *Collected Papers*, II, 286.
15. JONES, E. *Papers on Psycho-Analysis.* (Baillière, Tindall and Cox, 4th ed.; London, 1938), p. 520.
16. WORTIS, J. "Fragments of a Freudian Analysis," *American Journal of Orthopsychiatry,* 1940, 10:844-845.
17. LANDIS, C. "Psychoanalytic Phenomena," *op. cit.,* p. 21.
18. I have translated this from Freud's *Sammlung Kleiner Schriften zur Neurosenlehre.* (3te Folge, Leipzig and Wien, 1931), p. 88. My translation of this passage is more accurate, if less graceful, than the official rendering in Freud's *Collected Papers,* Hogarth edition, III, 246.
19. FREUD, S. *The Question of Lay Analysis.* (W. W. Norton and Company, New York, 1950), p. 25.
20. ———. *Ibid.,* pp. 82-83.
21. ———. *An Outline of Psychoanalysis.* (W. W. Norton and Company, New York, 1949), p. 77.
22. COHEN, M. R., and NAGEL, E. *An Introduction to Logic and Scientific Method.* (Harcourt, Brace and Company, New York, 1934), p. 325.
23. LANDIS, C. "Psychoanalytic Phenomena," *op. cit.,* p. 28.
24. FREUD, S. *Psychoanalysis: Exploring the Hidden Recesses of the Mind.* Translated by A. A. Brill, Encyclopaedia Britannica. Quoted in: BRILL, A. A. *The Basic Writings of Sigmund Freud.* (The Modern Library, Random House, New York, 1938), pp. 6-7.
25. ———. *A General Introduction to Psycho-Analysis,* p. 387.
26. ———. *The Question of Lay Analysis,* p. 83.
27. HINSIE, L. E., and SHATZKY, J. *Psychiatric Dictionary,* p. 532, "Transference."
28. FREUD, S. *A General Introduction to Psycho-Analysis,* p. 387.
29. ———. *The Question of Lay Analysis,* p. 82.

30. FREUD, S. *A General Introduction to Psycho-Analysis,* p. 386.

31. ———. *An Autobiographical Study.* (The Hogarth Press and The Institute of Psycho-Analysis, London, 1946), p. 76.

CHAPTER 4

Psychoanalytic Dream Interpretation

1. FREUD, S. "The Interpretation of Dreams." In *The Basic Writings of Sigmund Freud.* Translated and edited by A. A. Brill. (The Modern Library, Random House, New York, 1938), p. 391.

2. ———. *Ibid.,* p. 540.

3. The turn of phrase is from: WOHLGEMUTH, A. *A Critical Examination of Psycho-Analysis.* (George Allen and Unwin, London, 1923), p. 91.

4. LANDIS, C. "Psychoanalytic Phenomena," *Journal of Abnormal and Social Psychology,* 1940, 35:17-28.

5. WORTIS, J. "Fragments of a Freudian Analysis," *American Journal of Orthopsychiatry,* 1940, 10:845.

6. FREUD, S. "The Interpretation of Dreams," *op. cit.,* p. 339.

7. ———. *Ibid.,* p. 492.

8. ———. *An Outline of Psychoanalysis.* (W. W. Norton and Company, New York, 1949), pp. 56-57.

9. ———. "The Interpretation of Dreams," *op. cit.,* p. 234.

10. HINSIE, L. E., and SHATZKY, J. *Psychiatric Dictionary.* (Oxford University Press, New York, 1940), p. 172, "Dream, artificial."

11. FREUD, S. "The Interpretation of Dreams," *op. cit.,* p. 283.

12. ———. *New Introductory Lectures on Psycho-An-*

alysis. (W. W. Norton and Company, New York, 1933), p. 31.

13. ———. "The Interpretation of Dreams," *op. cit.*, p. 234.

14. ———. *New Introductory Lectures on Psycho-Analysis*, p. 42.

15. ———. *Ibid.*, p. 45.

16. ———. "The Interpretation of Dreams," *op. cit.*, p. 223.

17. ———. *Ibid.*, p. 276.

18. ———. *A General Introduction to Psycho-Analysis.* (Perma Giants, New York, 1949), p. 198.

19. ———. *Ibid.*, p. 75.

20. ———. *New Introductory Lectures on Psycho-Analysis*, p. 27.

21. ———. *An Outline of Psychoanalysis*, p. 61.

22. HALL, C. S. "What People Dream About," *Scientific American*, May, 1951:60-63. *See also* "Diagnosis of Personality by the Analysis of Dreams," *Journal of Abnormal and Social Psychology*, 1947, 42:68-79.

23. FREUD, S. "The Interpretation of Dreams," *op. cit.*, p. 539.

24. ———. *Ibid.*, p. 538.

25. JONES, E. *Psycho-Analysis.* (Cape and Smith, New York, 1929), pp. 64-65.

26. FREUD, S. "The Interpretation of Dreams," *op. cit.*, pp. 250-251.

27. ———. *Ibid.*, p. 392.

28. ———. *Collected Papers.* (The Hogarth Press, London, 1950), V, 155.

29. ———. "The Interpretation of Dreams," *op. cit.*, pp. 393-394.

30. ———. *A General Introduction to Psycho-Analysis,* pp. 136-137.

31. ———. *Collected Papers,* IV, 202.

32. FREUD, S. "The Interpretation of Dreams," *op. cit.*, pp. 390-391.

33. ———. *A General Introduction to Psycho-Analysis*, pp. 137-138.

34. ———. *Ibid.*, p. 138.

35. ———. *Leonardo da Vinci.* (Random House, New York, 1947), pp. 106-107.

36. ———. *A General Introduction to Psycho-Analysis*, p. 139.

37. ———. *Ibid.*, pp. 139-140.

38. ———. "The Interpretation of Dreams," *op. cit.*, p. 388.

39. ———. *Ibid.*

40. ———. *A General Introduction to Psycho-Analysis*, p. 140.

41. ———. *Collected Papers*, II, 287.

42. ———. *A General Introduction to Psycho-Analysis*, p. 140.

43. ———. *An Autobiographical Study.* (The Hogarth Press and The Institute of Psycho-Analysis, London, 1946), p. 84.

44. ———. "The Interpretation of Dreams," *op. cit.*, p. 392.

45. ———. *An Autobiographical Study*, p. 84.

46. ———. "The Interpretation of Dreams," *op. cit.*, p. 283.

47. HEALY, W., BRONNER, A. F., and BOWERS, A. M. *The Structure and Meaning of Psychoanalysis.* (Alfred A. Knopf, New York, 1930), p. 259. This is not a quotation from Jones. I am quoting Healy, Bronner, and Bowers.

48. SCHAFER, R. *Journal of Abnormal and Social Psychology*, 1950, 45, No. 1:187.

49. WORTIS, J. "Fragments of a Freudian Analysis," *op. cit.*, pp. 843-849.

50. FREUD, S. "The Interpretation of Dreams," *op. cit.,* p. 253.
51. ———. *Ibid.,* p. 376.
52. ———. *Ibid.,* p. 343.
53. LORAND, S. *Technique of Psychoanalytic Therapy.* (International Universities Press, New York, 1946), pp. 190-191.
54. FREUD, S. "The Interpretation of Dreams," *op. cit.,* pp. 391-392.
55. LORAND, S. *Op. cit.,* pp. 191-192.
56. FREUD, S. *New Introductory Lectures on Psycho-Analysis,* p. 23.
57. ———. *Ibid.,* p. 24.
58. HEALY, W., BRONNER, A. F., and BOWERS, A. M. *Op. cit.,* p. 277.
59. FREUD, S. "The Interpretation of Dreams," *op. cit.,* p. 390.
60. ———. *Ibid.,* p. 241.
61. ———. *Ibid.*
62. ———. *Ibid.,* p. 242.
63. FROMM, E. *The Forgotten Language.* (Rinehart and Company, New York, 1951), p. 92.
64. FREUD, S. *A General Introduction to Psycho-Analysis,* p. 141.
65. ———. "The Interpretation of Dreams," *op. cit.,* p. 383.
66. VELIKOVSKY, I. "The Dreams Freud Dreamed," *Psychoanalytic Review,* 1941, 28:487-511.
67. FREUD, S. *Collected Papers,* IV, 259-260.
68. ———. "The Interpretation of Dreams," *op. cit.,* p. 258.
69. WORTIS, J. "Fragments of a Freudian Analysis," *op. cit.,* p. 847.
70. FREUD, S. *An Outline of Psychoanalysis,* pp. 49-50.
71. ———. *Moses and Monotheism.* (Alfred A. Knopf, New York, 1949), p. 157.

72. FREUD, S. *A General Introduction to Psycho-Analysis,* p. 177.

73. ———. "The Interpretation of Dreams," *op. cit.,* p. 381.

74. ———. *An Outline of Psychoanalysis,* pp. 49-50.

75. ———. "The Interpretation of Dreams," *op. cit.,* p. 467.

76. HEALY, W., BRONNER, A. F., and BOWERS, A. M. *Op. cit.,* p. 448.

77. LANDIS, C. "Psychoanalytic Phenomena," *op. cit.*

78. SELLING, L. S. "Effect of Conscious Wish upon Dream Content," *Journal of Abnormal and Social Psychology,* 1932, 27:172-178. Quoted from:
   SEARS, R. R. *Survey of Objective Studies of Psychoanalytic Concepts.* Social Science Research Council, Bulletin 51, New York, 1943, p. 130.

79. FREUD, S. *New Introductory Lectures on Psycho-Analysis,* p. 25.

80. ———. *Collected Papers,* V, 141.

81. ———. *Ibid.*

82. ———. *A General Introduction to Psycho-Analysis,* p. 213.

83. ———. *Collected Papers.* V, 145.

84. ———. *Ibid.,* II, 311.

85. ———. *Ibid.,* p. 307

86. ———. *Ibid.,* p. 310.

CHAPTER 5

Psychoanalytic Normality

1. FREUD, S. *An Outline of Psychoanalysis.* (W. W. Norton and Company, New York, 1949), p. 53.

2. ———. *Collected Papers.* (The Hogarth Press, London, 1950), V, 327.

3. FREUD, S. *Ibid.,* p. 354.
4. ———. *Ibid.,* p. 341.
5. KUBIE, L. S. *Practical and Theoretical Aspects of Psychoanalysis.* (International Universities Press, New York, 1950), pp. 13-14.
6. FREUD, S. *Collected Papers,* I, 280.
7. MULLAHY, P. *The Saturday Review of Literature,* October 15, 1949:34.
8. FREUD, S. *Collected Papers,* V, 229-230.
9. ———. *New Introductory Lectures on Psycho-Analysis.* (W. W. Norton and Company, New York, 1933), p. 176.
10. ———. *Collected Papers,* II, 273.
11. ———. *Ibid.*
12. ———. *New Introductory Lectures on Psycho-Analysis,* p. 176.
13. HINSIE, L. E., and SHATZKY, J. *Psychiatric Dictionary.* (Oxford University Press, New York, 1940), p. 381, "Oedipus Complex, passing of."
14. FREUD, S. *An Outline of Psychoanalysis,* p. 97.
15. ———. *Collected Papers,* II, 273.
16. ———. *Ibid.*
17. ———. *An Outline of Psychoanalysis,* p. 81.
18. ———. "The Interpretation of Dreams." In *The Basic Writings of Sigmund Freud.* Translated and edited by A. A. Brill. (The Modern Library, Random House, New York, 1938), p. 381.
19. ———. *An Outline of Psychoanalysis,* p. 104.
20. ———. *Collected Papers,* V, 337.
21. ALEXANDER, F. See HEALY, W., BRONNER, A. F., and BOWERS, A. M. *The Structure and Meaning of Psychoanalysis.* (Alfred A. Knopf, New York, 1930), p. 299.
22. FREUD, S. *A General Introduction to Psycho-Analysis.* (Perma Giants, New York, 1949), p. 274.
23. Quoted in: LUDWIG, E. *Dr. Freud.* (Hellman Williams and Company, New York, 1947), pp. 131-132.

24. FREUD, S. *Collected Papers,* II, 388.
25. ———. *Three Contributions to the Theory of Sex.* (4th ed.; Nervous and Mental Disease Publishing Co., N. Y., 1930), p. 24.
26. ———. *Collected Papers,* IV, 49.
27. ———. *Ibid.,* p. 316.
28. ———. *Ibid.,* II, 243.
29. ———. *Ibid.,* p. 319.
30. ———. *Ibid.,* I, 344-345.
31. ———. *Ibid.,* p. 279.
32. ———. *The Question of Lay Analysis.* (W. W. Norton and Company, New York, 1950), p. 67.
33. ———. *Collected Papers,* I, 279.
34. ———. *An Autobiographical Study.* (The Hogarth Press, London, 1946), pp. 58-59.
35. Quoted in: LUDWIG, E. *Op. cit.,* p. 72.
36. FREUD, S. *Collected Papers,* II, 182.
37. ———. *Ibid.,* V, 266.
38. ———. *Ibid.,* III, 562-563.
39. ———. *New Introductory Lectures on Psycho-Analysis,* p. 139.
40. ORLANSKY, H. "Destiny in the Nursery," *Commentary,* June, 1948, 5, No. 6:563-569.
41. FREUD, S. *Collected Papers,* V, 90.
42. ———. *Ibid.,* II, 168-169.
43. ——— *Ibid.,* p. 45.
44. ———. *Ibid.,* p. 164.
45. ———. *Ibid.,* p. 45.
46. ———. *New Introductory Lectures on Psycho-Analysis,* pp. 138-139.
47. HEALY, W., BRONNER, A. F., and BOWERS, A.M. *Op. cit.,* p. 315.
48. FREUD, S. *Collected Papers,* III, 587.
49. GLOVER, E. *Freud or Jung.* (W. W. Norton and Company, New York, 1950), p. 92.
50. *See* WITTELS, F. *Sigmund Freud.* (Dodd, Mead and

Company, New York, 1924) . Wittels later published an abject retraction of this book. *See* "Revision of a Biography," *Psychoanalytic Review,* 1933, 20:361-374.

HITSCHMANN, E. "Freud in Life and Death," *American Imago,* 1941, 2:127-133.

LUDWIG, E. *Op. cit.,* particularly pp. 271-311.

PUNER, H. W. *Freud, His Life and His Mind.* (Grosset and Dunlap, New York, 1947) .

51. MACNAUGHTON, D. "The Inner World of the Preschool Child," *Child Study,* 1950-1951, XXVIII, No. 1:8.

52. FREUD, S. *New Introductory Lectures on Psycho-Analysis,* p. 203.

CHAPTER 6

Analysis Terminable and Interminable

1. FREUD, S. *New Introductory Lectures on Psycho-Analysis.* (W. W. Norton and Company, New York, 1933) , p. 207. This is the source of the first sentence. The rest is from Freud's *Collected Papers.* (The Hogarth Press, London, 1950) , V, 353. I have taken the title of this chapter from an article of Freud's, "Analysis Terminable and Interminable," in the same volume, pp. 316-357.

2. ———. *An Autobiographical Study.* (The Hogarth Press and The Institute of Psycho-Analysis, London, 1946), p. 71.

3. ———. *The Question of Lay Analysis.* (W. W. Norton and Company, New York, 1950) , p. 81.

4. ———. *Ibid.,* p. 77.

5. ———. *Ibid.,* pp. 76-77.

6. Freud discusses most of these forms of resistance. *See* HEALY, W., BRONNER, A. F., and BOWERS, A. M. *The*

Structure and Meaning of Psychoanalysis. (Alfred A. Knopf, New York, 1930), p. 447.

7. FREUD, S. *Collected Papers,* II, 318.
8. RIVIERE, J. *See* HEALY, W., BRONNER, A. F., and BOWERS, A. M. *The Structure and Meaning of Psychoanalysis,* p. 447.
9. FREUD, S. *Collected Papers,* V, 342.
10. ———. *The Question of Lay Analysis,* p. 81.
11. ———. *New Introductory Lectures on Psycho-Analysis,* p. 44.
12. ———. *An Autobiographical Study,* p. 51.
13. ———. *Collected Papers,* I, 297.
14. ———. *Ibid.,* p. 267.
15. ———. *Ibid.,* IV, 86.
16. ———. *The Question of Lay Analysis,* p. 48.
17. ———. *Collected Papers,* II, 362.
18. ———. *Ibid.,* p. 365.
19. ———. *Ibid.,* pp. 363-364.
20. ———. "Psychopathology of Everyday Life." In *The Basic Writings of Sigmund Freud.* Translated and edited by A. A. Brill. (The Modern Library, Random House, New York, 1938), p. 96.
21. ———. *Moses and Monotheism.* (Alfred A. Knopf, New York, 1949), p. 149.
22. SEARS, R. R. "Experimental Analysis of Psychoanalytic Phenomena." In *Personality and the Behavior Disorders.* Edited by J. McV. Hunt. (The Ronald Press Company, New York, 1944), I, 320.
23. ———. *Ibid.,* p. 329.
24. FREUD, S. *Collected Papers,* II, 396.
25. ———. *Ibid.,* p. 397.
26. ———. *Ibid.,* IV, 343.
27. DUNBAR, F. *Psychosomatic Diagnosis.* (Paul B. Hoeber, New York, 1943), p. 226.
28. ———. *Mind and Body.* (Random House, New York, 1947), p. 96.

29. GANTT, W. H. *Experimental Basis for Neurotic Behavior*. (Paul B. Hoeber, New York, 1944) , p. 102.
30. ———. *Ibid.,* p. 158.
31. FREUD, S. *A General Introduction to Psycho-Analysis*. (Perma Giants, New York, 1949) , p. 390.
32. ———. *Ibid.,* pp. 387-388.
33. ———. *Collected Papers,* II, 360.
34. ———. *The Question of Lay Analysis,* pp. 83-84.
35. ———. *Collected Papers,* II, 314.
36. ———. *Ibid.,* p. 290.
37. ———. *The Question of Lay Analysis,* p. 85.
38. ———. *Collected Papers,* I, 293.
39. Quoted in: PUNER, H. W. *Freud, His Life and His Mind*. (Grosset and Dunlap, New York, 1947) , p. 189.
40. FREUD. *The Question of Lay Analysis,* p. 84.
41. ———. *A General Introduction to Psycho-Analysis,* p. 386.
42. ———. *Collected Papers,* II, 380.
43. ———. *An Outline of Psychoanalysis*. (W. W. Norton and Company, New York, 1949) , p. 66.
44. ———. *An Autobiographical Study,* p. 74.
45. ———. *Collected Papers,* V, 358.
46. ———. *Ibid.,* p. 359.
47. ———. *Ibid.,* p. 360.
48. ———. *Ibid.,* p. 367.
49. ———. *Ibid.,* II, 360.
50. ———. *An Autobiographical Study,* p. 74.
51. WORTIS, J. "Fragments of a Freudian Analysis," *American Journal of Orthopsychiatry,* 1940, 10:843-849.
52. FREUD, S. *An Autobiographical Study,* pp. 72-73.
53. ———. *Collected Papers,* II, 18-19.
54. COLEMAN, L. R., and COMMINS, S. *Psychology*. (Boni and Liveright, New York, 1927) , p. 29.
55. FREUD, S. "The History of the Psychoanalytic Movement." In *The Basic Writings of Sigmund Freud,* p. 975.

56. FREUD, S. *Collected Papers*, I, 226.
57. ———. "The Interpretation of Dreams." In *The Basic Writings of Sigmund Freud*, p. 236.
58. ———. *Collected Papers*, I, 280-282.
59. ———. *Ibid.*, III, 137.
60. ———. *Ibid.*, IV, 348.
61. ———. *The Question of Lay Analysis*, pp. 53-54.
62. ———. *Collected Papers*, I, 79.
63. ———. *New Introductory Lectures on Psycho-Analysis*, p. 115.
64. ———. *An Outline of Psychoanalysis*, p. 85.
65. ———. *Collected Papers*, II, 300.
66. ———. *Ibid.*, V, 127.
67. ———. *Beyond the Pleasure Principle*. (The Hogarth Press, London, 1948), p. 1.
68. ———. *Collected Papers*, IV, 14.
69. ———. *An Outline of Psychoanalysis*, p. 29.
70. ———. *Ibid.*, pp. 85-86.
71. ———. *Ibid.*, p. 85.
72. ———. *Ibid.*
73. ———. *Ibid.*, p. 113.
74. ———. *Beyond the Pleasure Principle*, p. 17.
75. ———. *Collected Papers*, II, 288.
76. ———. *A General Introduction to Psycho-Analysis*, p. 392.
77. ———. *Collected Papers*, II, 362.
78. MEAD, M. "What Psychoanalysis Does for You," *Look*, September 26, 1950:114-122.
79. FREUD, S. *Collected Papers*, II, 50.
80. ———. *An Outline of Psychoanalysis*, p. 66.
81. HEALY, W., BRONNER, A. F., and BOWERS, A. M. *Op. cit.*, p. 370.
82. FREUD, S. Quoted in: *Ibid.*
83. ———. *New Introductory Lectures on Psycho-Analysis*, p. 118.
84. ———. *Ibid.*, p. 120.

85. HEALY, W., BRONNER, A. F., and BOWERS, A. M. *Op. cit.*, p. 314.

86. FREUD, S. *Collected Papers*, II, 220.

87. ———. *Ibid.*, IV, 132.

88. ———. *Ibid.*, V, 199.

89. ———. *The Problem of Anxiety.* (W. W. Norton and Company, New York, 1936), pp. 14, 15.

90. ———. *Collected Papers*, V, 38.

91. ———. *Ibid.*, I, 120.

92. ———. *Ibid.*, IV, 451.

93. ———. *An Autobiographical Study*, pp. 123-124.

94. ———. *The Problem of Anxiety*, p. 61.

95. ———. *Ibid.*, p. 39.

96. ———. *Ibid.*, p. 41.

97. ———. *Collected Papers*, V, 189.

98. ———. *Ibid.*, II, 50.

99. ALEXANDER, F. *Psychosomatic Medicine.* (W. W. Norton and Company, New York, 1950), p. 222. Alexander is referring to
    GERARD, M. W. "Enuresis. A Study in Etiology," *American Journal of Orthopsychiatry*, 1939, 9:48-58.

100. Quoted by HOLLINGWORTH, H. L. *Abnormal Psychology.* (Methuen and Company, London, 1931), p. 410.

101. LANDIS, C. "Psychoanalytic Phenomena," *Journal of Abnormal and Social Psychology*, 1940, 35:17-28.

102. FREUD, S. *Collected Papers*, II, 400.

103. WERTHAM, F. "What to Do Till the Doctor Goes," *The Nation*, September 2, 1950:205-207.

104. MILNER, M. "A Note on the Ending of an Analysis," *International Journal of Psycho-Analysis*, 1950, 31:191-193.

105. FREUD, S. *Collected Papers*, V, 320.

106. ———. *Ibid.*

107. ———. *The Question of Lay Analysis*, pp. 86-87.

108. REICH, A. "On the Termination of Analysis," *In-*

ternational Journal of Psycho-Analysis, 1950, 31:179-183.

109. FREUD, S. *The Question of Lay Analysis,* p. 97.

110. MYERSON, A. "The Attitude of Neurologists, Psychiatrists and Psychologists toward Psychoanalysis," *American Journal of Psychiatry,* 1939, 96:623-641.

111. WERTHAM, F. "What to Do Till the Doctor Goes," *op. cit.,* pp. 205-207.

112. STRAUSS, E. B. "Quo Vadimis," *British Journal of Medical Psychology,* 1947, 21:1-11.

113. KNIGHT, R. P. "Evaluation of the Results of Psychoanalytic Therapy," *American Journal of Psychiatry,* 1941, 98:434-446.

114. KESSEL, L., and HYMAN, H. T. "The Value of Psychoanalysis as a Therapeutic Procedure," *Journal of the American Medical Association,* 1933, 101, November 18:1612-1615.

115. APPEL, K. E. "Psychiatric Therapy." In *Personality and the Behavior Disorders.* Edited by J. McV. Hunt. (The Ronald Press Company, New York, 1944), II, 1107-1163.

116. ———. *Ibid.,* p. 1155.

117. ESTES, S. G. *The Journal of Abnormal and Social Psychology,* 1947, 42:141.

118. SALTER, A. *Conditioned Reflex Therapy.* (Farrar, Straus and Young, New York, 1949.)

119. SNYGG, D., and COMBS, A. W. "The Phenomenological Approach and the Problem of 'Unconscious' Behavior: A Reply to Dr. Smith," *The Journal of Abnormal and Social Psychology,* 1950, 45:523-528.

120. JAMES, W. *Principles of Psychology.* (Henry Holt and Company, New York, 1890), I, 534, 549. (Reprinted, Dover Publications, 1950.)

DATE DUE